the Yoga of the three ENERGIES

james swartz

Yogaland Limited

Published by Yogaland, 1 Lilley Mead, Redhill RH1 2NY
www.yogaland.co.uk

A paperback original

ISBN 978-0-9956889-1-9

Printed by Biddles Books, King's Lynn, Norfolk PE32 1SF

Contents

Introduction

UNTIL THE INDUSTRIAL Revolution survival dictated the way we lived, women married to raise children and men more or less did what their fathers did. Life was hard but simple. The Industrial Revolution created sufficient wealth to allow large middle classes to develop in Western countries, but the need to survive still kept societies conservative; men were taught the trades and entered the working class or went on to "higher" education and enjoyed middle-class family life. Women were housewives. Other options were few. Yes, you could live on the fringes of society, but very few enjoyed a temperament that immunized them against the social opprobrium that accompanied alternative lifestyles. The rich of course lived their cliché as always, devoid of the imagination required to move beyond their conditioning. The post-World-War-II economic boom, however, created sufficient wealth to present alternative lifestyle options to an ever-increasing segment of the population. A significant fraction of middle-class youth, subjected to the particular malaise that accompanies mind-numbing materialism, rebelled. In the argot of the sixties, they "turned on, tuned in and dropped out." The beatniks of the fifties pried the lifestyle door open a crack, and in the sixties hippies pushed it wide open. It was no longer necessary to keep one's nose to the grindstone to survive and live the humdrum lives of Mom and Pop; there was sufficient wealth to insure food and a roof over one's head, if you didn't mind a little inconvenience. Peace and wealth provide the luxury necessary to ask questions.

Chapter I

Success

IF YOU ASK one thousand people if they want to fail in life, you will not receive one affirmative response. Conversely, if you ask if someone wants to succeed, you will only get an affirmative response. And if you ask for a definition of success, all replies will boil down to one: success is "getting what I want." Furthermore, we should probably illumine the implied meaning of this definition: success is also "avoiding what I don't want." It's never more complex than that.

We Are Not Complex

From childhood we want to succeed. Success, however, is not a foregone conclusion, because the desire to succeed does not generate the situations that conform to our desires and fears, likes and dislikes, preferences and aversions. Life's seeming indifference to our likes and dislikes creates a lot of emotion. We get angry when it does not conform to our wants and we become euphoric when it does. Both anger and euphoria lead to depression, a feeling that "life has let me down." Somehow we find ourselves bouncing back and forth between these two poles, although if the media is a reliable guide, it seems most of us spend more time down than up.

It is fashionable among the educated to imagine that our emotional problems are due to complexity, but they aren't. We are not complex. Emotionally we are not different from children. Children make a big fuss when they don't get what they want. The only difference between us and them lies in the fancy stories we concoct to justify our emotionality. Kids are more transparent.

Our tales of hardship and woe play well with others, up to a point. But overdo them and they depress even the sunniest personality. The complexity argument serves to keep us in the dark concerning the absolute simplicity of our problems.

Of course we don't want to blame ourselves for our emotionality, because it has become part and parcel of who we are. Back in the day it was shameful to go on about one's problems. While the stiff upper lip is preferable to the wailing and gnashing of teeth that passes for civil discourse these days, it too is unbecoming. When you can't honestly look at yourself and admit that you are a big baby emotionally, you need rationalizations or you need to blame somebody or something. That something is usually life itself. The argument, which is not profound, often goes something like this: "Life is too complex; it is going too fast. What can one do?" It's a depressing argument. In fact life is not complex and it is not going fast. Our minds are just a big mishmash of rapidly moving thoughts, and our emotions follow suit.

All rationalizations are questionable. Complexity and time are thoughts that hide the basic fact that we do not understand ourselves as we are and we do not understand the nature of the field of existence into which we have been unceremoniously thrust.

Let's assume that there is nothing wrong with needing things and with the expectation that life should give us what we need. Insofar as we didn't come here on our own, isn't it reasonable to expect life to feed us at least? It is probably not unreasonable to expect a roof over our heads as well, a cardboard box under a freeway off-ramp as a bare minimum. Life seems to have a more or less endless supply of clothing, so we're good to go. More things or events do not equal complexity, although the belief that it does obscures the elegant simplicity of life's inherent order.

"Chaos" is one of the favorite keywords of the complexity theory, "random" is another. Life is not chaotic or random. It may seem so to a mind that has incomplete information and reduced powers of observation, but life is intelligently designed. It is a field of physical, psychological and moral laws.

Before we continue, let's review the basics. One fine day I appear here in my birthday suit through no fault of my own. I want things and I expect life to give me things. Getting what I want and not getting what I want justifies my emotions. Behind this notion of entitlement is the presupposition that life is in a position to give me what I want. But is it? Does life have the same degree of masturbatory self-regard toward me as I have toward myself?

It should be obvious to anyone that the fundamental difference between me and life is the fact that I only have to look after myself, but life has to look after everything. In a way, there is a similarity because I have to look after the objects in my environment that are important to me, basically people, so I have to take their needs into account when I want something from them. Remember, I always want something, and everything I get comes from someone or something else: a group, a social, governmental, business or religious institution. I am totally dependent on life.

The Needs of the Total Come First

The basic difference, however, is this: life does not depend on me. It has a rather more extensive brief. Since everything depends on it, it has to look after everything. If you want to get a handle on your emotions, learn this *mantra* and repeat it religiously every time you beg the world to satisfy your desires: THE NEEDS OF THE TOTAL COME FIRST.

Appreciating this fact should calm you down a bit and help you appreciate another inconvenient truth: life is not here to give us want we want, only what we need. In case you find this fact disconcerting, you need to consider an obvious difficulty that your demands cause.

Let's say both you and someone else want to marry the same person or two football teams pray to the same God for victory – what's God supposed to do? Since life sees no difference between you and anyone else, who should be rewarded? There is a law that takes care of this kind of problem, but it is not a law that is universally appreciated.

Let's state the obvious because it is seemingly not obvious: this is a lawful universe. When you are too tightly cocooned in your petty fears and desires, you are not interested in laws. You want what you want the way you want it and you want it now. In fact rules become irritants when you have strong fears and desires, and although you may not break them, you are sorely tempted to do so. In case it never occurred to you, desire is not necessarily your friend.

The entertainment age is in full swing, and we expect to be entertained more or less constantly. We are happy to park our empty minds in front of digital devices of all ilk and let the internet do the work, but Vedanta is not passive entertainment. It is a provocative method of self-inquiry that requires considerable thinking. It is formulated in Sanskrit and contains a few key concepts that have no equivalents in other languages, although they can easily be explained in English. So to take full advantage of this wonderful teaching, please commit to memorizing a handful – about twenty – words. You won't regret it. Vedanta is scientific inquiry into existence and brilliantly explains three basic topics: consciousness, the world and the human mind with reference to the idea of happiness.

Human beings have one extremely tedious and glaring fault: they always have an agenda. They have little appreciation of things as they are and are simultaneously cursed with an insatiable need to sell something, usually themselves, in one way or another. We want others to think we are unique and specially gifted in ways too numerous to mention. What you are about to discover is not mine; it comes to me from an impeccably impersonal source, about which much can be said, but which will become apparent as I present this great knowledge for your edification and upliftment.

What Is *Dharma?*

The first word you need to remember is *dharma*. It has several meanings. The first is "appropriate response." *Dharma* is not a magical formula like the famous "Secret" that took the spiritual world by storm some years ago. It will not instantly open the gates to heaven.

If you are not clear that there is always an element of uncertainty concerning the results of your actions, you are pretty thick. It is quite reasonable to think that life is fickle, but the fact that we do not always get what we want, and often get what we don't or nothing at all, is not evidence of unreliability. But it is a fact that unless you respond to life's demands with the appropriate action at the right time, you will not succeed. For instance, if you show up for a job interview on Friday when your appointment was for Thursday, you will definitely not get the job. If you show up drunk on Thursday and tell the interviewer that you don't care for her hairdo, you will not get the job. And you may show up on time, properly prepared, put your best foot forward and still not get the job. All is not lost, however, because if you do everything humanly possible you will not be tempted to think of yourself as a failure. You can legitimately blame the situation.

The second *dharma* intimately involved in action is *svadharma*, your nature. We are all programmed to respond in a certain way. Business types look to make a buck in every situation, helping types to make things better, and criminals need to break the rules. All living beings invariably follow their natures – dogs don't quack and ducks don't bark. Because humans, however, are capable of introspection, they can become aware of their natures and if they don't like the way they are programmed they often try to be someone else.

Acting out an idea that is not in harmony with your program is unwise. If you do, life will not bless you with success. You are here to work out your *karma* as you are, whether you like yourself or not. If you do so properly, you will end up liking yourself a lot.

The third concept of *dharma* is *samanya dharma*, the universal moral laws built into reality. *Samanya dharma* is based on the non-dual nature of reality and is responsible for the fact that there is a universal expectation of non-injury. Even hitmen carry guns to protect themselves, and thieves lock up their loot. I don't lie to you, because I don't like to be lied to. If you don't take universal values into account, you will definitely reap a lot of pain from your interactions with the world.

The fourth *dharma* factor is called *visesa dharma*. *Samanya dharma* is absolute values, but life is not black and white; it is shades of gray. *Visesa dharma* is situational ethics, how we interpret absolute values. It is pesky to apply because every situation we face requires a tailored response. Dogs bark at everyone, the man carrying a stick and the woman bringing it a bone. It's okay for dogs because they are not trying to be happy, but barking at everyone who invades your space is not a winning strategy. In general, I should tell the truth, but how much truth do I tell – all of it, a lot, a little bit, not too much, an alternative fact, a white lie, a bald-faced lie? It is not always clear.

Finally, there is the Self, *Dharma* with a capital "D." The Self is your existence/awareness, that because of which you exist. Let's call it the "real you." If you act without awareness of this factor, you will not be satisfied even if you get everything you want in life. If your life is dedicated to understanding and actualizing your true Self, it can be a raging success.

At the end of the day, you want to look back on your life and say that it was successful and enjoyable. Sometimes we get what we want but at such great cost to ourselves and others that we end up exhausted, bitter and lonely. So a truly successful life is a well-lived life, one that enjoys its strivings, flows naturally around obstructions and eventually actualizes its goals.

Your Primary Instrument

We have two basic tools for achieving success, a body and a mind, which we call the "subtle body." The subtle body is our primary instrument, and the physical body is secondary. Of course we can't accomplish anything without a physical body, but the subtle body controls the physical body, so it is called the "primary instrument." If your primary instrument is knowledge-based and takes *dharma* in all its nuances into account, it will not worry about what has been done, what is being done now and what needs to be done later. Worry, the signature energy of humans, is a killer, a death of a thousand cuts. Every little worry inevitably takes its toll, slowly sapping your vitality, etching lines of suffering in your face, robbing your step of its spring, gradually sabotaging your health, hollowing out your interior until you are little more than an empty, diminished version of yourself. It will send you to an early grave. It is a dull knife incapable of cutting away life's detritus. Shorn of worry and inspired by a great idea, your mind is your best friend.

The Value of Goals

Sad to say, your primary instrument does not do well on its own. Left to its own devices it is like a needy, untrained puppy, sniffing here and there looking for amusement. If it isn't properly disciplined, it will poop anywhere, bark anytime, eat the most disgusting things, tromp across the carpet with muddy feet and contaminate your bed with its stinky hair and body odors. Yes, it's a loveable little creature, but it will dog you mercilessly and sit at your feet begging for attention until the cows come home. It needs something to do, but what?

There are seemingly lots of options, but there is actually only one option masquerading as two. The world, the *dharma* field, is a combination of spirit and matter, about which much will be said later. "Spirit" is a term that lends itself to vague meanings. We call it ever-free, ever-present existence/awareness, or existence/consciousness. It is a self-evident fact that we exist and that we are conscious. This "spiritual" Self does not change. The material portion of the world is opposite the spiritual portion. It changes, has attributes and is never free. It is completely dependent on the spiritual Self, existence/consciousness. Both principles are eternal. They have no beginning.

Because we are part and parcel of the *dharma* field, we are confused. The question "Am I am a spiritual being or a material being?" is the basis of most internal conflict, yet it is rarely appreciated as such. Although it is not obvious, the mind is a material instrument too. It is just subtle matter, inert material waves that endlessly appear in the form of the fears and desires motivating our actions. If I'm my body-mind, there are many things I can pursue, the most obvious of which is security.

Pleasure-seekers are materialists too; they need to satisfy the cravings of their material selves. They obviously don't know who they really are, because the Self, consciousness, is free of desire. Without much inquiry it becomes apparent that most other human pursuits – power, fame, etc. – can be reduced to the need to secure a place for the body-mind entity in the material world and entertain it once it is secure.

At the same time, the consciousness portion, which is our essential nature, creates a powerful need for freedom. Freedom from what? Freedom from dependence on material things, subtle and gross. We know this because every human action is an attempt to rid oneself of a sense of limitation. I don't actually want what I think I want – a subtle object, like a feeling – or a situation, like a job or a marriage – or a gross object, like a house or a car. I want freedom from want because accommodating that needy little dog within is painful. It is never satisfied. You can throw your fears in with your desires because they are non-separate; a desire is a positive fear and a fear is a negative desire. One is always lurking behind the other.

Contrary to conventional wisdom, our wants create shattered minds and miserable lives. We know this because we want what we want for happiness, not for the ostensible objects of our desires. Why? Because we stop wanting when the desired object is attained and we become happy. And when we are happy we don't want our desires/fears to come back and mar our perfect satisfaction. Happiness is the experience of our whole and complete, blissful, conscious Self that happens when wants and fears are suspended. So even materialists with their myriad pursuits are, unbeknownst to them, seeking freedom.

A few of us – seekers, or inquirers if you prefer – march to the tune of a different drummer, however. We feel the call of freedom directly and pursue it according to our lights. Our primary drive is to understand things, not to possess things. Yes, we have our material wants, but they play second fiddle to the desire to know who we are, how the world was created and the answers to any number of other existential questions. Materialists sometimes become inquirers when they realize that seeking objects for happiness is a zero-sum game. Every upside has its downside. No matter how many of your desires you satisfy, the desires keep coming, usually until the day you die. In fact you don't want to die, because you believe that there is still something to be attained while you're here.

This elegant spartan logic should lead to the following conclusion: if I want freedom – which I do if I am a conscious human being – I need to know which part of myself is spiritual and which part is material. If I am clear on this issue, I will not identify with my material portion, because doing so will keep me in bondage to things. Conversely, I will identify with the spiritual portion because it is always free.

The problem is not complicated, nor is the solution. However, solving the problem is not easy, because I have been conditioned since birth to identify with the material portion, courtesy of Mom and Pop, who standing at the bottom of an endless chain of moms and pops, tend to be in thrall to the material portion alone. Freedom is not their strong suit, so they make sure we identify with our bodies and pursue material ends.

How could they make such an obvious mistake? The body is an inert object, and I am a conscious subject. Even babies know their bodies are objects. We can't say that babies know who they are, except perhaps by default, but they know who they aren't because they treat their bodies as objects. Once Mom and Pop get done with you, however, you are convinced you are the body. So you're setting out in life in a leaky boat.

Although getting what you want is up to life, what you want is up to you. You can indirectly gain momentary freedom by acquiring certain things – security, pleasure, power, fame, knowledge, etc. – or you can go directly for freedom.

If you know that the pursuit of material ends is characterized by stress and worry born of uncertainty, and that the pursuit of your spiritual Self is characterized by an ever-expanding sense of peace and uncaused happiness, the choice should be a no-brainer.

So to keep my needy little dog, my primary instrument, from driving me crazy, I need to give it noble work, to wit: I need to teach it how to inquire into who it is. Sadly, suffering does not tend to lend dispassion to the mind, although occasionally it does, so we immediately start seeking answers without actually knowing how to inquire. Not knowing what we really want, apart from a vague idea of enlightenment, we dive into the spiritual world without so much as a by-your-leave. No wonder we end up disappointed or worse: we fall prey to one of the myriad charlatans promising instant *nirvana*. It is not the intention of this book to expose the many enlightenment myths lurking like crocodiles in the muddy waters of the modern spiritual world, although I am duty-bound to deal with the most obvious. If you are new to seeking, please read Chapter II of *How to Attain Enlightenment: The Vision of Non-Duality* or *The Essence of Enlightenment: Vedanta, the Science of Consciousness* to understand the fallacy behind most enlightenment teachings.

This book presents one of the most interesting and sophisticated teachings of Vedanta, the Yoga of the Three Energies. It is not a *yoga* that involves twisting your body like a pretzel in 110-degree heat or prancing around in Lycra spandex tights to bless others with spectacular views of your gluteus maximus. It is knowledge *yoga* and it clarifies the relationship between you and your material portion, and it shows you how to inquire.

Inquiry is not innocently pestering the Void with the "who am I?" question and waiting for a reply from a transcendental deity. It is the application of the knowledge of existence/consciousness, your true identity, to the many confusing emotion-laden situations that regularly bedevil your primary instrument. It is, contrary to popular opinion, using the primary instrument, not denying or destroying it, to creatively separate your material self from your spiritual Self, which will eventually result in permanent freedom, assuming you vigorously commit yourself to it. Please don't complain that inquiry is difficult. It is as difficult as you want to make it. If you understand its value, it is a great pleasure from start to finish. If not, not.

If you don't know who you are and you let your desires run amok, that cute little puppy turns into a raging, muscular Rottweiler and ends up menacing and controlling you. If you do know who you are, you can easily control your mind. It's that simple. What you probably don't know is that your thoughts, and the feelings they cause, are not etched in stone. They seem to be involuntary because they just won't go away. But they will go away if you bump them out with true thoughts that inspire and uplift the mind – until the true thoughts become second nature. True thoughts are happiness-producing thoughts that represent your highest value and invoke your higher nature.

In any case, the topic of this chapter is success, which was defined as getting what you want. Assuming that you don't already have what you want, your primary instrument is the means of attainment. It is the means for experience and knowledge. Since life is nothing but experience and knowledge, you are stuck with your primary instrument. Don't expect some *guru* to rescue you.

The question then becomes: What kind of knowledge and experience do I want? Since reality has a spiritual and a material part, I need knowledge of both. Pursuing worldly knowledge alone will not solve my problem. My emotional side will grow like a weed and choke out all noble impulses. If I focus solely on my spiritual side, I will likely end up floating in the ether with the angels or subjecting my self-esteem to immeasurable diminishments at the hands of self-appointed, ego-busting *avatars*. So the only solution is to get complete knowledge of the nature of reality. The Yoga of the Three Energies is a complete, time-tested, scientific teaching on the nature of reality.

Material Reality Is Three Energies

The material part of reality is controlled by three energies (*shaktis*). These energies are called "*gunas*," a Sanskrit word that means "qualities" and "ropes." From the macrocosmic point of view, they are attributes or qualities found in everything, but when we take the microcosm into account they are ropes that bind us tightly to our material side. All three of these energies are necessary and useful – they completely define us as living beings – but any one of them can create problems.

When we are ignorant of our spiritual nature – ever-free consciousness – we are particularly susceptible to the downside of each energy. The subtle body, our primary instrument, is completely under the influence of these three powers until we set it free. We cannot attain success without understanding these three forces and the techniques that transform them.

Success in any field, worldly or spiritual, depends on the relative proportion of each with reference to the energy dominating an individual's mind and his or her environment at any moment. If this statement seems a little abstract, don't worry. We will presently flesh it out in great detail.

Subject-Object

Before we proceed, we need to present an important definition that lies at the heart of all Vedantic teachings: subject-object. To understand the distinction between the subject and objects is *guna* transcendence, liberation. It is not merely an intellectual appreciation of the distinction but an ongoing, immediate, palpable, experiential appreciation of the blissful freedom of the subject.

However, to gain transcendence, we need to intellectually appreciate the nature of the subject and the nature of objects so it is clear which subject has a *guna* problem and which doesn't. It's a tricky business because there is actually only one subject appearing as two. And the second subject, which we think is us, is actually an object!

Until the last chapter, which reveals the nature of liberation in light of the life of the second subject, this book basically addresses the life of the second subject as it is now because the second subject is bound by the *gunas,* not free of them.

Who Is the Second Subject?

The second subject is the person that we have been conditioned to think we are by society. Not to put too fine a point on it, it is the person on your driver's license, the one that was born at a certain time, has certain physical and psychological characteristics and that will eventually die one day. This person is not actually a subject. It is an object. How it gets to be an object is explained in Chapter IV.

The original subject, hidden from the second subject behind a wall of ignorance, is the true Self, pure awareness/consciousness. The purpose of the *guna* teaching is to reveal the original real you, which, you will be happy to know, will make the "second you" a very happy person.

To return to the teaching: life is an ever-changing, apparently conscious subject, which I think of as myself, interacting with a field of ever-changing, inert objects, which I think of as not-me. Both the field and the conscious subject are nothing but the three *gunas* because the Creation itself is nothing but these three basic energies. I feel the need to apologize for this strange word, but as the teaching unfolds you will see why there is no equivalent in any language, insofar as it encompasses every known object in existence, including the word "energy" owing to the way our minds think about it.

It is very difficult to see asphalt, for instance, as energy, although it is. It is almost impossible to see that it isn't separate from me. We get a little help from quantum mechanics in this regard, which points out that life as we know it is energy, but quantum mechanics doesn't help us to understand our minds and emotions, which are also only energy. We can't expect material science to know consciousness either, because it is beyond energy.

The *gunas* are not conceptual; they are the immediate experience of everyone and part and parcel of everything. This teaching helps you identify various energies, monitor them and transform them so that you can achieve your goals.

In any case, wouldn't you think that any attempt by an ever-changing entity to find lasting happiness in an ever-changing field of energy is a foregone conclusion? The best-case scenario is a few blips of happiness when the subject and object fortuitously collude and, sadly, equal blips of misery when they collide.

The pursuit of material goals demands a different *guna* set from the pursuit of spiritual goals. Since this book is written for people whose stated aim in life is freedom from dependence on objects, it touts the development of the quality that makes knowledge possible, since the only way to freedom in this energy matrix is through self-knowledge.

This is not to say that *guna*-knowledge does not apply to the pursuit of worldly goals – security, pleasure, virtue, fame, power, etc. – it is very useful. So if you are a materialist at heart, don't stop reading. In fact wherever you find a successful worldly person, the success is due to the confluence of an individual's subjective *guna* make-up and the *guna* composition of his or her environment. The success is usually fortuitous, however, not the result of a conscious application of knowledge, because worldly people are not aware of their unconscious motivations.

Freedom, however, is not a happening, since the Self is already free. Even in the case of the person who claims to have been set free by grace without inquiry or the hard work that leads to inquiry, a careful analysis of the individual's subjective make-up will reveal that an unconscious operation of *guna*-knowledge somehow manifested as "enlightenment."

Sad to say, the spiritual world has always been burdened with the notion that, since the Self is already accomplished, nothing can be done to accomplish it. Consequently many seekers, owing to intellectual sloth, are content to wait for "grace," the likelihood of which is considerably less than winning the lottery. Yes, the Self is already accomplished, but the fact that an individual is seeking freedom means that the Self is not known for what it is.

This situation is rather like individuals who seek love from people who are seeking love, since the likelihood of finding it is virtually nil insofar as neither person knows what love is. To those who tout grace as a solution, it should be known that even Ramana Maharshi, the most famous non-achiever of enlightenment in recent memory, exclusively promoted self-inquiry as a means of enlightenment.

In any case, once you understand the science of energy, you can earn all the grace you need. Enlightenment is not about getting a special experience that will purportedly solve all problems. Enlightenment is shedding ignorance and its effects. And since ignorance and its effect – the belief that your beliefs, opinions, prejudices, judgments, biases, etc. is actually knowledge – is hardwired, how likely is it that one fine day in the not too distant future you will wake up totally free and totally satisfied with who you are and with the life dictated by your *karma*?

Whether you like it or not, your self-esteem will grow by leaps and bounds if you assign your primary instrument, which needs worthwhile work anyway, the task of gaining this most beneficial knowledge. We are not saying that you won't be in a position to retire from action one day because your true nature is actionless awareness. Oddly, your primary instrument is capable of transcendence, but not by zipping off into some special transcendental sky. Transcendence requires preparation. This book presents the knowledge required to prepare you for freedom.

A Successful Life Requires an Enlightened Lifestyle

An enlightened lifestyle helps you quickly and efficiently achieve your goals, spiritual or material. Non-conforming lifestyles prevent success. It is amazing that people toil ceaselessly and unsuccessfully in their chosen fields for years but do not see the connection between the way they live and their lack of success. Everyone has a value for health, but the lifestyle of choice in modern materialist societies is inimical to this value. Only after sixty years is the public beginning to suspect that the mindless consumption of processed food coupled with sedentary lifestyles is related to health issues too numerous to catalogue. Diseases of civilization, like diabetes, cancer and AIDS, unknown in traditional cultures until recently, are exclusively transmitted by lifestyle.

Chapter II
How *to* Achieve Success

YOU ACHIEVE SUCCESS by managing your energy. Whether you pursue security, pleasure, virtue, fame, power or liberation, you need a dedicated *guna*-managed lifestyle. To achieve an appropriate lifestyle, you need to *guna*-manage your mind. To manage your mind, you need *guna*-knowledge.

Blaming yourself for failures and taking credit for successes is a problem because it makes everything that happens about ME, as if I were the only object in existence. Yes, I do exist and I play a part in life, but anyone with a modicum of smarts can see that I am only one small factor in a vast web of relationships that extends far beyond my immediate environment. So carrying the burdens of the world makes me a burden to myself and others.

Guna-knowledge, knowledge of the big picture, is the solution because it lays the responsibility for what happens to me – good and bad – elsewhere and moves me from the center of my life to the periphery, where the view is much more realistic.

It relieves the performance anxiety and allows me to completely relax in otherwise stressful situations. And it is equally good for the world because it greatly improves my cranky, dissatisfied personality and turns me into an asset in the eyes of others, which bodes well for success.

Getting Along with Yourself

Understanding the *gunas* not only optimizes chances of success in the world, it optimizes chances of a successful relationship with yourself. Since you play an important role in your success, it behooves you to get along nicely with yourself. Inner conflict compromises your primary instrument and renders it unsuitable for actualizing your goals. Self-obsessed individuals are not generally happy people.

Of course you care about yourself, but if you are too self-centered you will give the world short shrift, and since the world is the other half of the life equation, it will undoubtedly return the favor. So how does *guna*-knowledge solve this problem? It depersonalizes your relationship to yourself and to life in general.

This statement may seem strange because for most of us personal uniqueness is the essence of our identities. Our total insignificance in a world of seven billion creates an obsessive desire to stand out. Behind this need, perhaps because of it, is a simple fact: we are not unique at all.

Because we come from the same source, we all have the same equipment, the same feelings and emotions, and the same dreams and aspirations. In fact the more unique I feel the more problems I encounter because differences strain easy communication and efficient action.

And it should not be lost on anyone seeking success that everything we want comes from others. If we share a common identity, communication is simple. If we choose to atomize ourselves with exclusionary concepts, we are asking for trouble. To get what I want I need to accommodate myself to life, but specialness infects me with the vain belief that the world should accommodate itself to me. The duckling that refuses to stay in line quickly becomes food for the eagle. It is not a compromise to fit in; it is common-sense wisdom.

The Cosmos Becomes a Chaos

Obviously, the world is just an impersonal field of forces, laws and principles that serves, but is not set up to pander to, individuals. A beautiful verse in Handel's *Messiah* says the "Lord," meaning the field of life, "makes the rough places plain." It is the great leveler. The cosmos becomes a chaos the minute it breaks its own rules to accommodate uniqueness. If life was personal, nobody would get out of bed in the morning, because purposeful work would be impossible. Success is possible precisely because life is impersonal. Understand the laws and forces, and creatively interact with them, and you will achieve more or less predictable results. You can only bend reality to your will if you appreciate the impersonality of everything.

The more special you think you are, the more you dislike yourself too because you are more difficult to please. You can never eat the same meal tomorrow or wear the same outfit today that you wore yesterday.

You quickly tire of the color of the walls and the predictable demands of your friends. Unlike us, animals are okay with themselves and with other members of their species because they have no way to compare themselves to others. Yes, disassociation from life based on childhood trauma is an unnatural condition, but non-comparative depersonalization is not a pathology. It is a healthy state of mind based on an acute appreciation of the nature of reality.

Doership

Understanding the *gunas* solves another big problem: doership. Because of a seemingly inviolable link with the physical body, everyone automatically thinks of himself or herself as a doer. The doer has one simple brief: to become an enjoyer. It does actions to enjoy results that it believes will bring happiness. If you are already happy, you may do various activities but you do them happily, not for happiness. In this case the results of your actions are not a source of stress. But if you need something to happen to feel good, you have a problem, because there is always a gap between the action and the result.

Yes, you need air to feel good, but air is always present, so no anxiety is associated with breathing unless your lungs are inefficient. But when you demand scarcer objects – a good job, for instance – you run into trouble. Scarce objects tend to be more valuable because the demand for them outstrips the supply. If a relatively valuable object – a beautiful, sexy, rich, educated man or woman in a three-story McMansion in a gated community – is required to make you happy, you will suffer stress in direct proportion to the scarcity of the object, your means to attain it and the intensity of your desire for it. There is no actual logic behind the stress, because the result you want is not up to you, assuming you have done the appropriate actions, but it is painful to be separated from what you actually want, access to the unalloyed happiness that is your Self.

Perhaps not, but don't you ever tire of being you? If it doesn't bore you silly to listen to yourself air the same tired complaints, rationalizations, justifications and excuses to shore up your self-esteem, it should. Or if it doesn't, you probably love yourself unconditionally, which is good – or you are merely brain-dead. Nearly everyone wishes they were a more, better or different self precisely because being a doer/enjoyer entity is extremely tedious at a minimum and often painful in extremis. Manage the *gunas* and you will wake up as a fresh new self every day because you will be growing, not stagnating like a potted plant. Your story will become interesting and you will become a scintillating personality.

What Are the *Gunas?*

Life is an unbroken stream of daily situations dictated by our *karma,* and the *gunas* create the states of mind with which we try to manage them.

Did you ever wonder why you are either (1) tired, fuzzy-minded, lazy, depressed and confused, (2) stressed, frustrated, disturbed, scattered, restless and unfocused or (3) happy for no reason, blissful, still, focused, dynamic and creative? The answer: the *gunas* created these states.

Did you ever wonder why you can feel quite lovely when you start the day but feel uncomfortably sad later, external factors remaining the same? Sometimes you feel quite agitated and a few minutes later you feel pleasantly high, external factors remaining the same. The *gunas* are forces that make you think what you think and feel what you feel without asking your permission.

One of the rules for writing scripture is to explain the benefit or benefits of a particular teaching. I think I have covered the main point sufficiently, but it bears repeating. If you manage your *gunas*, life will flow nicely and you will feel good about yourself. You may not get everything you want, but you will be quite okay with what happens. Before we discuss the origin of this knowledge we need to make an important point: everything you do from dawn to dusk is *guna*-management; you just don't know that is what you are doing.

When you're hung-over after a hard day's night and you guzzle a double espresso, you are managing a *guna*. When you kick back with a couple of beers and a cheesy pepperoni pizza after a hard day's work, you are managing a *guna*. When you turn on the TV, you are trying to change your state of mind. When you get drunk or smoke some dope, you are managing your *gunas*. When you pay your insurance, you are managing a *guna*. Sex is *guna*-management. Everything we do is an attempt to improve our state of mind. Or to put it negatively, nothing we do is intended to create an uncomfortable state of mind.

So what is the problem? Why not just let things happen as they do and call it a day? Because things are not set up to make us feel good. If the doer knew who it was, it would not feel the need to change its state of mind. Wouldn't it be nice if what happened really didn't matter – but in a good way? If the doer could manage his energy properly, he would basically enjoy a pleasant state of mind most of the time and would possess enough skill to prevent negative thoughts from becoming negative states of mind.

If the doer knew what it was doing, it would do the appropriate actions at the appropriate time and, assuming the field of life was in a good mood, which it generally is, the media's carefully selected negative view to the contrary notwithstanding, we would mostly have everything we want and would mostly be happy. But the doer isn't in control of its feelings, because it doesn't understand them.

Feelings recycle automatically according to the law of *karma*. In an attempt to change them, the doer tries what didn't work before, thinking that it will produce a different result the next time, a popular and eminently reasonable definition of insanity if ever there was one.

If you are plagued by a negative mind, it may seem as if it isn't your own doing, but it is, particularly if you are *guna*-educated and understand how *karma* works. Please don't try to wiggle out of this indictment with the spiritually fashionable claim that you are not the doer, so what you feel doesn't matter. It is always the doer that says it is not the doer, and bad feelings always matter to it. Uttering the statement "I am not the doer" without a complete understanding of the nature of the *guna* field is simply denial.

The Origin of *Guna*-Knowledge

Guna-knowledge is based on careful observation and analysis of experience. Our states of mind are perceived objects known to us. From an analysis of their effects, we can confidently determine their nature. Samkhya, one of the six orthodox Vedic schools that developed several centuries before the Christian era, is the first to mention this knowledge. Because Vedanta has no quarrel with knowledge gained by observation and inferences drawn from experience, the *gunas* have become an important teaching. We find them mentioned in the scriptures on *dharma* and further developed in the *Bhagavad Gita*. In fact the *Bhagavad Gita*, which is a scripture on *dharma* and liberation, is organized on the *guna* model.

Chapter III

Creation

THIS TECHNICAL CHAPTER is very important because it reveals the subtle process that creates the world and human beings.

If you want to understand why you experience what you experience with the idea of gaining power over your life, you need this knowledge. Sanskrit terminology is included after the English definitions. This teaching is very ancient but appears more recently in *Panchadasi*, a fourteenth-century text, and is sourced in the *Upanishads*. *Panchadasi* is available from ShiningWorld as a paperback entitled *Inquiry into Existence: The Lamp of Knowledge*.

Existence/Consciousness Exists Prior to the Creation

Because the world evolved out of existence/consciousness and because there are not two existences, what we experience here has always been here. The power in existence to create is called *Maya*. It creates the world out of existence. *Maya* is primordial matter and the intelligence that shapes it. It is grosser than existence but subtler than the forms that evolve out of it. It is inert and capable of reflecting awareness. It is made of three elemental energies or powers: *sattva*, *rajas* and *tamas*. Each energy has a particular quality, or *guna*. These energies are everything, are in everything and create everything.

Normally, the creator and the substance out of which it creates objects are different. A potter, for instance, is different from the clay out of which the pot is created. But existence is non-dual consciousness, so there is not another substance from which *Maya* can create.

So it fashions the Creation out of itself just as a spider generates its web out of its own body. Therefore the substance of all objects is consciousness. To design something requires intelligence and ideas. For the same reason that matter is consciousness transformed by *Maya*, intelligence and knowledge are also consciousness; there is no other option. The spider's mind creates the web. And the spider has the power to transform itself into its web without ever ceasing to be a spider! Consciousness appears as this world without undergoing any change.

1. Pure Reflected Consciousness

Creation takes place in three stages. During the first stage, pure reflecting consciousness, *sattva*, is dominant. It is awareness appearing as a knower. It is omniscient and is the blueprint for the eternal truths, forces and laws that structure the Creation, the three *gunas*, the five elements, the living beings and *karma*. It is called *Isvara*. In religious terminology, it is God. *Isvara* is consciousness identified with everything. Original pure consciousness identifies with nothing.

2. Consciousness Reflected: Dull Mirror

In the second stage, the *sattva* recedes and macrocosmic *rajas* dominates. During this stage, *rajas*, the projecting power, and *tamas*, the concealing power, muddy the pure mirror of matter. *Rajas*, the "Big Bang," causes *avidya*, self-ignorance, and then shatters the mirror of material awareness into innumerable shards, scattering them throughout the Creation. These shards reflect awareness in the form of infinitely diverse living beings. When you see a living being, you see reflected consciousness and a material body.

As a result of the action of *rajas*, limitless awareness appears as a reflected, limited entity. It is called *Pragna Jiva*, the Eternal Individual. This *jiva* identifies with the reflecting medium, its subtle body, which is made of *sattva*, and accounts for the belief that it is a conscious being in its own right, whereas the consciousness it enjoys actually belongs to original pure consciousness.

The *jiva* is multifaceted and complex due to the many possible combinations of *sattva*, *rajas*, *tamas* and the Five Sheaths, which have many parts. Because *sattva* is contaminated with *rajas*, the *jiva's* knowledge is mixed with ignorance. *Jivas* are full of misconceptions. The *jivas* cannot be separated from the reflecting medium, the subtle body.

Ignorance (*avidya*) is the causal body. It hides awareness from the *jivas* and causes them to feel incomplete. At the same time, it projects enticing objects that *jivas* believe can complete them.

3. Non-Reflecting Consciousness: Predominant *Tamas* – The Black Hole

In this stage *Maya* manufactures matter out of *tamas*. If it manufactured matter out of *sattva*, we would see consciousness reflected in material objects, but matter absorbs rather than reflects consciousness. It is a "black hole." Matter is one eternal substance, but it evolves.

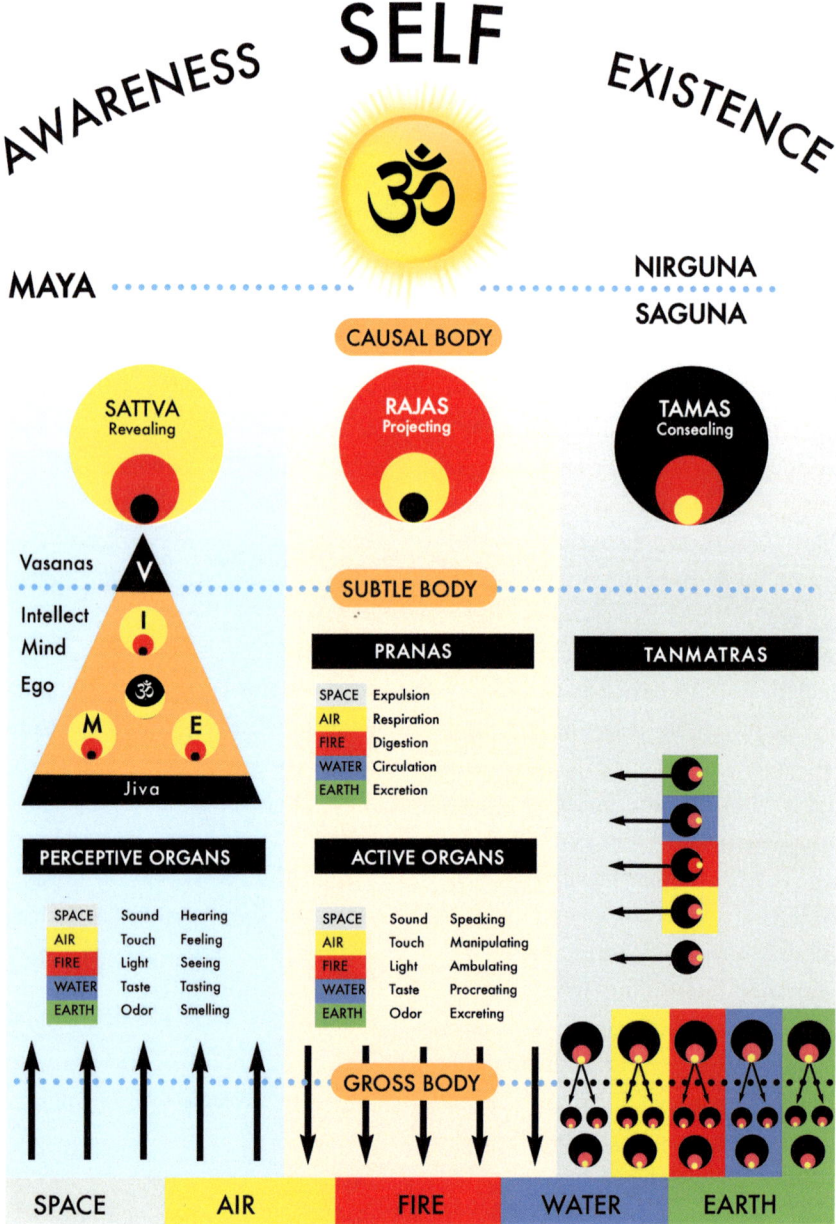

The Evolution of Matter

The Five Subtle Elements (space, air, fire, water and earth) arise from the part of primordial matter in which *tamas* predominates. Matter is inert. It can't do anything, because *rajas* is suppressed. It can't think or feel, because *sattva* is suppressed. It is meant for our experience. The world is not for *Isvara's* experience, because *Isvara* is not an individual with desires and fears that create good and bad *karma. Isvara* has no *karma.*

The Five Perceptive Organs: hearing, touch, sight, taste and smell evolved from the *sattva.* From the *tamasic* portion of the Five Subtle Elements, the organ of inner experience arose. It is the reflecting medium for consciousness, not the reflection itself. The organ of inner experience is called the subtle body, or mind, or primary instrument, and is made of many parts.

The Creation teaching is not meant to cement clever concepts about the precise structure of Creation in our minds, only to point out the fact that the Creation is a set-up. The perceptive organs gather information from the material world. The *sattva* manifests as three powers in the subtle body: it doubts, determines and acts. Its doubting function is called mind. Its determining, discriminating, analyzing, inquiring functions are called intellect. The third element of the subtle body is the doer. It is the power in us that causes action.

The organs of action evolve from *rajas* in a telescoping manner from subtle to gross: first speech, which is a property of the space element; then the hands, which come from the air element; the feet from the fire element; the sex organs from the water element; and the nose from the earth element. The organs are in the subtle body, their instruments are in the gross body.

Prana, the vital air sheath, also arises from the *rajas* portion of the Five Subtle Elements. It divides into five physiological functions: respiration, excretion, assimilation, circulation and the power to eject unwanted objects, which evolve out of their corresponding subtle elements.

The five sensory organs, the five organs of action, the five vital airs, mind, intellect and ego together form the subtle body. The subtle body cannot be perceived by the sense organs. It is made of *sattva* and reflects awareness. It is subject to change as the *gunas* modify it.

Macrocosm and Microcosm

To provide individual *jivas* with objects of enjoyment and make their bodies fit for enjoyment, *Isvara* causes each of the subtle elements (space, air, fire, water and earth) to share a fraction of themselves with each other. Consciousness plus the causal and subtle bodies are not sufficient for experience. Experience requires material elements and a gross body. The sense organs, which are in the subtle body, minus the physical sense instruments, are useless for creating and exhausting *karma.* Once the Creation gets to the subtle stage, *Isvara* is obliged to create gross elements out of the subtle elements and fashion physical bodies out of them so the *jivas* can work out their *karmas.* This is accomplished by a process called *panchikarana,* a fivefold division and

combination of the subtle elements.

The physical body is a counter across which *jiva* transacts its business with the world. *Isvara* is pure original consciousness plus pure *sattva*, so it enjoys itself by itself without the aid of sense organs, sense instruments and sense objects. *Jivas* under the spell of self-ignorance enjoy and suffer intermittently as *rajas* and *tamas* intermittently obscure the *sattva* in their subtle bodies. More or less constant enjoyment is possible if an individual's subtle body is predominately *sattvic*. When the subtle body is dominated by *rajas* and *tamas*, more or less constant misery is an individual's lot.

Dividing each subtle element into two equal halves and again dividing half of each into four equal parts, *Isvara* mixed the subtle elements so that the resulting gross elements contain half of their original natures and a one-eighth portion of each of the other four. The division of the elements accounts for the diversity of objects. All gross objects are alloys.

This is the cause-and-effect teaching, the idea being that the effect – what we experience here – is just *guna* energy in a particular form. The idea is to train your mind to see though the gross and subtle material coverings to the *guna*.

The *guna* itself is not particularly interesting unless you are trying to transform your mind, in which case it is essential knowledge, but if your aim is to transcend the *gunas*, the presence of the *gunas* implies existence/consciousness, your true Self, because the *gunas* arise out of *Maya/Isvara*, which is consciousness, your true Self. So in this way you can understand that everything you experience is you and set yourself free of bondage to matter. If matter depends on you, not you on it, where's the bondage?

The division and recombination of the subtle elements to produce physical matter is not the end of the Creation sequence. There's still a way to go until we see human beings talking on their smartphones.

From these composite elements the "cosmic egg" arose, and from it evolved all the worlds, the objects of experience and the bodies in which experience takes place. The "cosmic egg" means that the material Creation appears in an elliptical shape. It is Big-Banged out of a "black hole," or macrocosmic *tamas*, the densest matter. It is so dense that even light can't escape it or reflect off it.

Matter organizes itself according to instructions in the *sattva* into innumerable suns, planets and galaxies, which provide innumerable fields of experience, that is to say reflecting media, in which innumerable conscious beings – reflections – evolve bodies and minds, which live, reproduce themselves and die.

The only conscious beings of interest to us, however, are human beings. In the third stage of Creation, humans appear. They appear as an eternal individual first in the form of the deep-sleep entity. The deep-sleep entity morphs

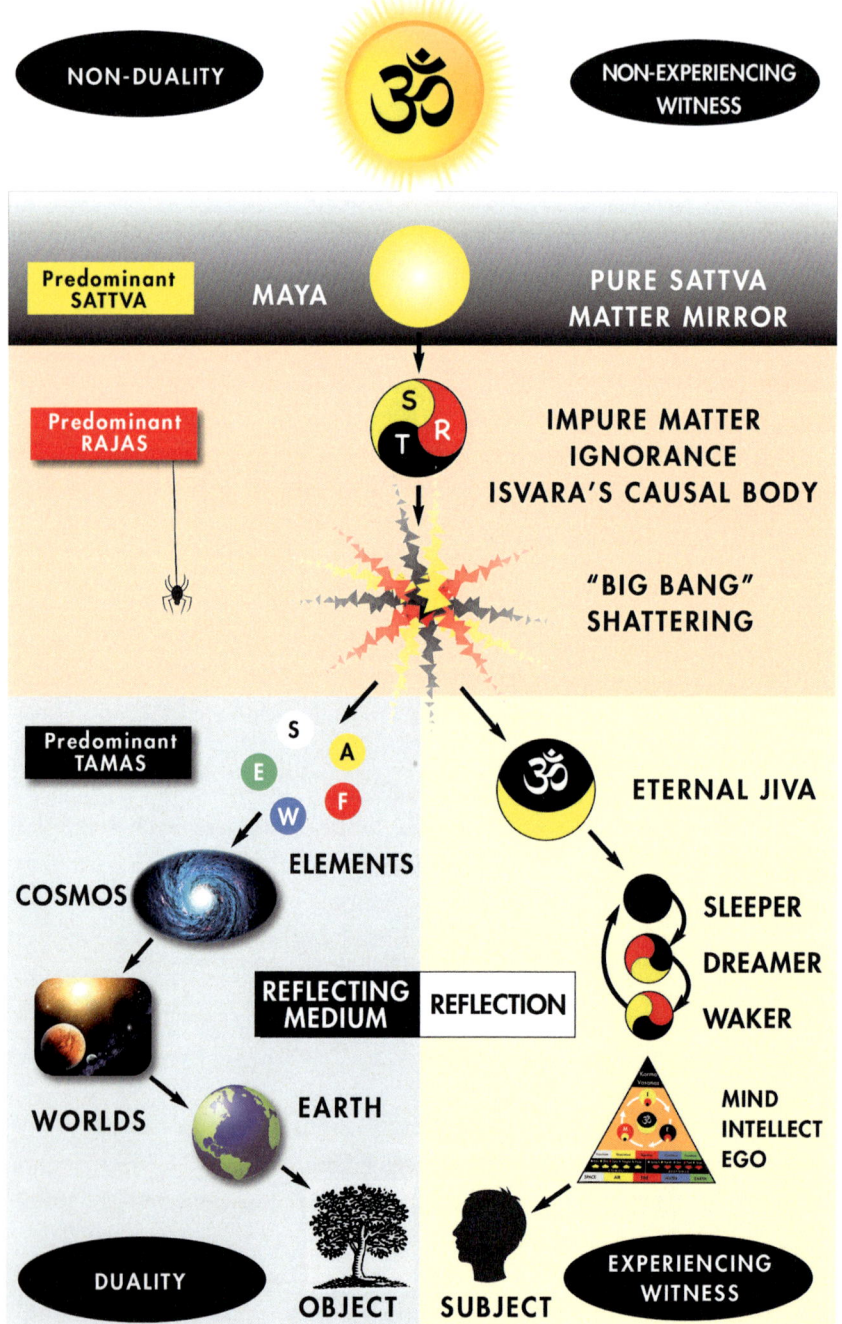

into a dream-state entity when *Maya* projects the subtle body. Finally, when the waking-state entity's *karma* kicks in, the dreamer changes into the waking-state entity, which begins immediately working out its *karma* in the waking state with the aid of its primary instrument, whose powers we have discussed above. The dream state entity does not create or exhaust *karma,* only the waker does. Waking-state entities seem to be unique, but they aren't; they all only wake, sleep and dream. In the waking state they create and exhaust *karma* endlessly unless they wise up.

Now the Creation is complete. Experience is consciousness appearing as an intelligent conscious entity transacting with a material field with the aid of a material reflector, the subtle body.

This teaching shows that we are a part of a conscious Creation, that we are not self-created, that our destiny is determined by *Isvara,* unless we take it into our own hands, and that our *jiva*-selves are nothing but the three *gunas.*

Chapter IV
The Microcosm ~ *The* Jiva: Ropes

BEFORE THE ETERNAL *Jiva* identifies with its primary instrument, the subtle body, the *gunas* are just qualities or energies. But once identification happens, they become binding. They don't bind *Isvara*, the Creator, but they bind *jiva* because, as mentioned above, the subtle body is subject to change as the *gunas* modify it.

Identification means that the *jiva* thinks that it is the subtle body, even though it isn't. It's a pure reflection of existence/consciousness, non-separate from it, just as the light of the moon is non-different from the light of the sun. Because it is so closely identified, however, it thinks that it thinks and feels, and it builds a story about what has happened, what is happening and what should happen to it. It is perennially bedeviled by a sense of helplessness, which manifests as a sense of low self-worth. Deep within it somehow knows that it is free and powerful, but it doesn't feel free and powerful, because the *gunas* are dictating every thought and feeling. In this way limitless, experience-free existence/consciousness "becomes" an experiencing entity.

The *jiva* is called the "I" sense. Just as the macrocosmic *gunas* reflect in the microcosmic subtle body, the limitless, non-dual Self reflects in the microcosmic subtle body as the Eternal *Jiva*. It cannot change its qualities, only the *guna* balance, the relative proportions of each. To change its qualities *Isvara* would have to invent other qualities, which is not going to happen. Nothing new comes into the Creation from elsewhere, because there is nowhere else.

The non-eternal *jiva* is the "second subject" mentioned above. It is pure original consciousness, the pure reflection and the reflecting medium, its *gunas* and *karmas*. It is the person you have been conditioned to think you are. It exists and experiences, but it is not real.

The Creation does what it is supposed to do — apparently cause a lot of trouble for *jivas* — but not really, because it is actually perfect as it is. This fact becomes known when the *gunas* become a springboard from which the *jiva* can disassociate from them. The *gunas* are like stepping stones. You start out in *tamas*, and with the help of *rajas* work your way out of it, which allows you to hop to *sattva* from which, to use a third metaphor, you leap beyond, as a pole-vaulter uses a pole to cross the bar. These are nice metaphors, but don't take them literally. You are not going anywhere. Transcendence, crossing the *Maya* bar, is not an action. It is understanding the nature of the *gunas* with

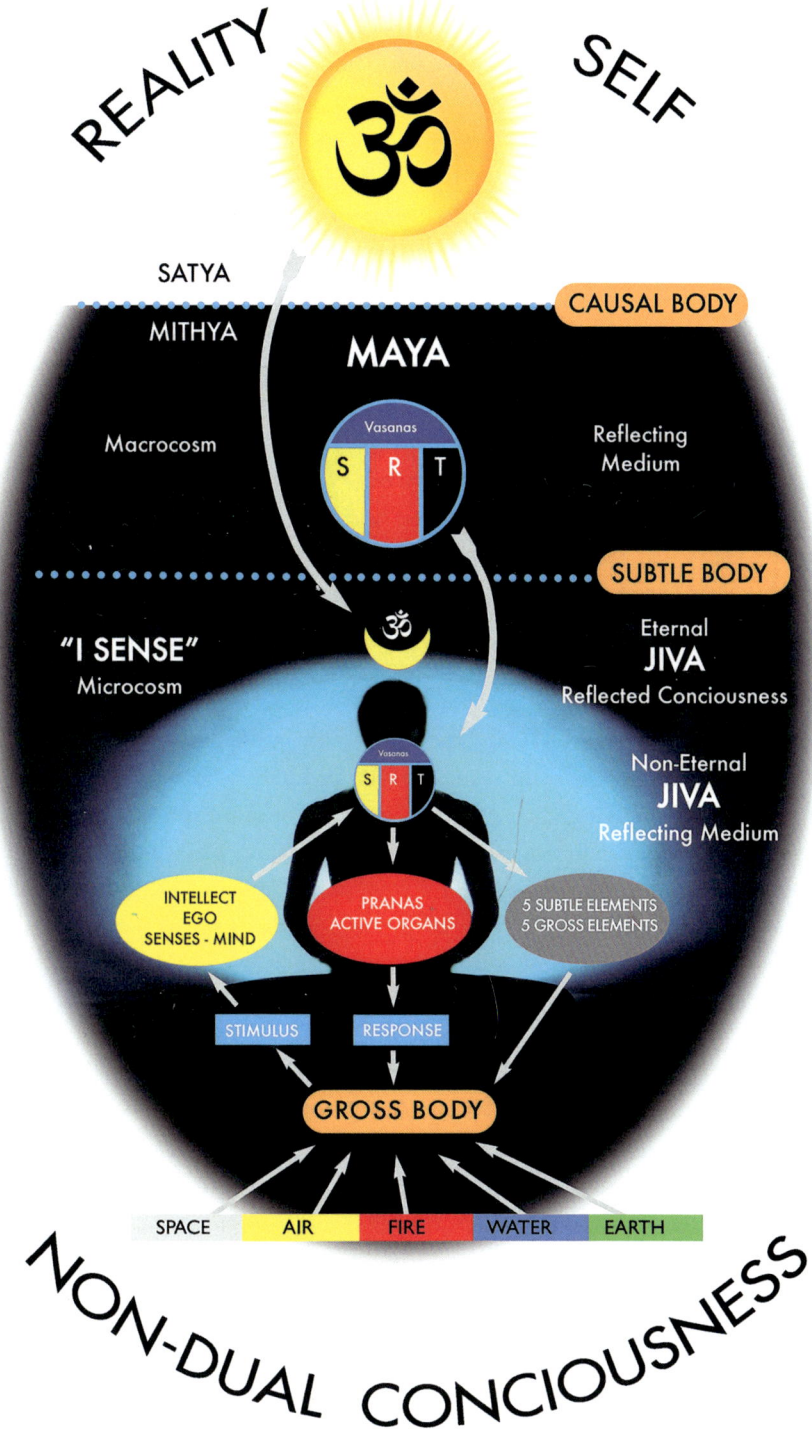

REALITY

SELF

SATYA

CAUSAL BODY

MITHYA

MAYA

Vasanas

S R T

Macrocosm

Reflecting
Medium

SUBTLE BODY

"I SENSE"

Microcosm

Eternal
JIVA
Reflected Conciousness

Vasanas

S R T

Non-Eternal
JIVA
Reflecting Medium

INTELLECT
EGO
SENSES - MIND

PRANAS
ACTIVE ORGANS

5 SUBTLE ELEMENTS
5 GROSS ELEMENTS

STIMULUS

RESPONSE

GROSS BODY

SPACE   AIR   FIRE   WATER   EARTH

NON-DUAL CONCIOUSNESS

reference to the witnessing principle, and identifying one's Self as the witnessing principle.

Because the witness is *guna*-free, enlightened people have no quarrel with the world. In fact the world is a beautiful reflection of the beauty that they are. For them it exists as an amusing, variegated, ever-changing bauble, but it might as well not exist insofar as it does not change them whatsoever.

No *guna* itself causes pain or pleasure, suffering or joy, a sense of limitation or liberation; these feelings only come about through our relationship with them. The *gunas* are natural states of experience. They are only good or bad insofar as they bless us with success or run afoul of our expectations, our likes and dislikes, and bless us with misery.

For instance, you wanted to perform well on a test. Unfortunately, the night before you partied with your friends, your mind was dull as a loaf of bread the next morning, and you failed miserably, which means that you are going to fail the class and will not graduate as planned. You will have to remain in school for another semester, which completely ruins your plans, including your engagement to the girl of your dreams who is not going to be amused by your antics.

Can you legitimately blame *tamas* for your anger and the subsequent depression? The *guna*-driven law of *karma* is totally indifferent to your desires.

If you needed a different result, you should have studied the day before, gone to bed early and got up rested in *sattva*, in which case your knowledge would have been at your fingertips and you would have aced the test. It's a no-brainer, except it isn't if your subtle body is sunk in *tamasic* sloth and your self-esteem is so low that you can't say no to your friends when they want to party. The lesson: there is nothing wrong with any *guna* or combination of *gunas*, only your inability to manage them.

So What Do the *Gunas* Do?
Objective Factors

1. The *gunas* structure society. You may think that modern democracy has rendered the class system obsolete, but you would be wrong. Class transcends politics. All societies are organized on a *guna* basis. The *gunas* create archetypes that function together to create social cohesion.

Intelligentsia: Every society needs values and ideas to survive. So *Isvara* creates an intelligentsia, individuals with predominant *sattva* backed by *rajas* and very little *tamas*, to facilitate its needs: priests, thinkers, scientists, inventors, artists, teachers, storytellers, entertainers and educators.

Administrative and professional class: To administer social, political and economic structures, enforce its values and implement its ideas, society needs a professional class: politicians, police, military, doctors, lawyers, etc. This class is characterized by predominant *rajas* backed by *sattva* (helping, serving, protecting, preserving) and a little *tamas*.

Commercial class: Societies need to create wealth, which requires predominant *rajas* characterized by vital, aggressive, greedy, materialistic individuals with a large dollop of *tamas* and some *sattva*. This class is selfishly active, the administrative and creative class – entrepreneurs, farmers, investors, etc. – not so much.

The working and service class: Societies need worker bees, predominant *tamas* mixed with *rajas* and very little *sattva*. Socially and politically conservative, the people in whom *tamas* predominates, are unimaginative and not prone to taking initiative. They are loyal to a fault and excessively stubborn.

2. The *gunas* control life cycles and rites of passage. *Tamas* rules the first two years of life. *Rajas* slowly takes over and carries you into adulthood when either *tamas* or *sattva* starts to predominate. If *sattva* predominates, you will grow spiritually. If *tamas* predominates, you will grow old and tired.

3. The *gunas* control the shape of your body and your health. They control the autonomic nervous system and all physiological processes, your biorhythms, sleep, sexuality and other activities.

4. The *gunas* create the circumstances of your birth. You should have been born to rich, educated, popular parents in an upscale neighborhood. Instead, you were born to uneducated hillbillies addicted to methamphetamines. You lived in a trailer on a hillside and grew up on white bread and Coca-Cola. Your health started failing when you were a teenager.

Or maybe you were born into a family of good, religious people, married well and raised a lovely family yourself. Whatever the set-up, you didn't choose it. You can imagine that in some past life you did something good or bad and your present situation is a reward or a punishment, but you can't recall doing anything in a past life that would explain your present circumstances. This is so because the "you" that you imagined you were before is not present in this birth. You don't know if you existed before, and there is no point in thinking about it, because you weren't; the *gunas* put you right where you belong.

5. The *gunas* control your associations with people. Individuals congregate on the basis of similar *guna*-influenced tendencies.

The Subjective Factor

1. The *gunas* control the changes in the primary instrument, the subtle body. The subtle body is the instrument of experience and knowledge. It seems as if we experience objects "out there in the world," but we don't, we experience them subjectively. Because reality is non-dual, there is no space or time, although *Maya* creates a false sense of dimensionality. The world appears in the subtle body as experienced knowledge. The subtle body appears in the Self as an instrument of experience and knowledge. So actually everything is experienced in the Self, and everything that is experienced is only the Self experiencing itself.

Basically nobody knows this fact, because the *gunas* make the subtle body look like it is something other than the pure reflected consciousness that you are.

To the degree that one identifies with one's thoughts and feelings, one is incapable of objectifying the mind and remains stuck in the world of duality. Once childhood pain has been resolved by *karma yoga* or some other means, it is possible to become objective about your thoughts and feelings and see that your primary instrument is controlled by the *gunas*, which makes transcendence possible. Transcendence is non-dual vision, benign indifference to experience and freedom from dissatisfaction-induced action. It is knowledge that the *jiva* has nothing to gain by doing things, but it is not inactivity. It is freedom in action, not freedom from it. Transcendence of the *gunas* is the topic of the final chapter. In the meantime, however, we need to learn how to identify the *gunas* with reference to their effects so we can use this knowledge to our advantage.

2. The *gunas* create your personality and lifestyle. *Sattva* inclines the mind toward knowledge, pleasure and beauty, and creates a knowledge-centric infrastructure for your life. If you enjoy solitude and simplicity, know that *sattva* is your dominant *guna*. It also creates an agreeable, accommodating personality because *sattvic* individuals are self-contained and self-satisfied.

Rajoguna inclines an individual to innumerable activities. It makes the mind restless and disturbed. Unless a person under the spell of *rajas* is dissatisfied, he or she is not satisfied. It creates complex, often overwhelming and unwieldy life situations. It creates outgoing, competitive, aggressive, power-hungry, needy personalities. Because desire is pain, it creates perverted personalities, sadomasochists and martyrs, for instance. Martyrs and masochists are not happy unless they are suffering, so with the aid of *sattva* they figure out creative ways to enjoy the pain.

Tamas inclines the individual to sloth because it suppresses *rajas* and *sattva,* creating a heavy, procrastinating mind and dark, loveless environments, ideal for inactivity. It evolves uninteresting, clueless personalities. A mind mired in fantasies, positive and negative, is *tamasic.* Fantasy, a compensatory mechanism, allows you to accomplish in your mind what you are too lazy and incompetent to accomplish in the real world.

3. *Vasanas, gunas* and *samskaras:* the *vasanas* are not actions, they are the tendencies that create action. They program us to behave in predictable ways. They are hidden in the subconscious mind, the causal body, but they appear in the subtle body as the thoughts and emotions that make up our everyday experience. If you want to change your behavior, you need to work with your thoughts because your thoughts turn into *vasanas* once they leave your mind. Because they are stored in the causal body, and the causal body is the three *gunas,* each *vasana* has a typical *guna* "color." *Sattva* colors the *vasana* with satisfaction, *rajas* with dissatisfaction, and *tamas* with sloth. When the mind is in the grip of *tamas,* you are probably too dull to know what you are thinking and feeling and/or too indifferent to care if you do know. This is not to say that a *tamasic* mind is not painful, but it takes pain for granted because it doesn't have enough *sattva* to look into it or enough *rajas,* dissatisfaction, to address it.

Gunas subsume *vasanas,* so if you can manipulate the proportions of causal *rajas* and *tamas* with reference to *sattva* by changing your thinking, you can reduce pain and dissatisfaction and increase your sense of satisfaction.

Samskaras are agglomerates of *vasanas* that produce distinctive patterns of thought, emotion and behavior. They cause archetypes and stereotypes. Astrology, the enneagram and psychology are rudimentary attempts to analyze these patterns.

The Sanskrit terms are creeping in like fog on a fall morning, and maybe you're starting to think that Vedanta is just too difficult. It would be a mistake to run with that thought. Life is words. Words got you in trouble in the first place, and you need words that take you where you need to be. These well-chosen, revealing words are part of Vedanta's plan to open wide a window on the secret of your existence, so commit them to memory. You won't regret it.

4. The *gunas* change predictably. They are the wheel of time. A *guna*-driven person is time-conscious. Someone who has transcended the *gunas* enjoys a spontaneous life of leisure irrespective of their transactional circumstances. The global wheel of time turns ceaselessly in the causal body as the three *gunas* revolve, an irresistible force causing you to act. If you've ever had the feeling that you are a puppet on a string, you now know why.

PREDOMINANCE

Although the three *gunas* are always present, *Maya* causes one *guna* to predominate at any time. When one *guna* is dominant, its effects manifest and the effects of the other *gunas* recede into the background.

If you are extremely busy for eight hours or more, *rajas* is predominant. You may be a dynamic bundle of flowing energy when you start the day, but by midday you will notice your energy start to flag. You may keep working at a high pace because you are on a schedule, but you will notice resistance. You think you made the schedule, but you didn't. *Rajoguna*, desire, wrote it from start to finish and compelled you to follow it. In any case, the resistance is *tamas* inevitably creeping up, getting ready to dominate *rajas*. By dinner time you have slowed down considerably because *tamas* is getting stronger. It is painful to fix dinner because it requires more *rajas*. You order a pizza. This is not true, *tamas* ordered a cheesy pepperoni pizza, its signature food, which throws a wet blanket on the fire of *rajas*, particularly if you've been ordered by the Beer God to swill it down with a couple of brews. Once the kids are in bed, there may be a momentary window of peace when *sattva* peeks through to illumine your life with a few minutes of pleasure at the hands of your favorite novel, but either *tamoguna* pulls you into the arms of Morpheus for a good night's sleep or *rajas* sneaks in with a fear-thought and keeps you up half the night worrying about – what else? – the future.

Within the seventy-five-year block of global time the *gunas* allot you for this incarnation, *rajas* creates a fluctuating sense of daily time. *Rajas* is action, and action is the way the doer generates events that produce the objects that are intended to relieve its desire and make it feel momentarily feel good.

Because reality is non-dual, there is no separation between the subject and the objects, and there is no separation between you and what you want. You are what you want, a statement that sounds like complete gobbledygook to worldly people.

If you think about it, there is no time when you do one action. Nor is there time when you do a subsequent action, because there is no way to measure the interval between the first and the second action. However, when you do the third action, there is a way to measure the interval between the first two. The doer always feels the pressure of time because it is remembering past actions and dreaming of future actions so it can say that so much "time" has passed.

But so what? What does it mean to say that an hour has passed? What does it feel like? It feels like pressure, stress, because all the doer's actions are related to manifesting something it doesn't have. So time is just a conceptual way to describe stress, which is just desire to have a certain result. This kind of time is very fickle. When things are manifesting smoothly, owing to the subjective *guna* combination that is appropriate for the objective circumstances, time flies, but when your *gunas* don't match the situation, the object of your desire is nowhere to be seen and time hangs heavy on your hands. Two hours watching a good movie passes quickly; two minutes in a torture chamber is an eternity. When your primary instrument is *tamasic*, you are too lazy to chase objects, so you aren't time-sensitive. It may take you a few days to realize that you missed an important appointment. When your mind is *sattvic*, you enjoy yourself irrespective of what you are doing, so time doesn't mean anything. You are aware of the world of time and keep your appointments, but there is no stress, because you are self-satisfied and well-organized.

5. The *gunas* bind: in the macrocosm the *gunas* are beautiful qualities; they create the world and the *jivas*, but at the Creation stage there is no one except *Isvara*, pure non-dual existence/consciousness, and *Isvara* is unaffected by the *gunas*. Additionally, duality has no meaning in the macrocosm, so there is no bondage. But once the Creation Big-Bangs, matter starts to evolve and the *jivas* appear, you have duality and with duality you get bondage in spades.

In fact everything in the apparent reality is bound tightly to everything else. See how intimately *rajas* and *tamas* are bound together, and how securely the *jiva* is tied to *rajas* and *tamas*. I've painted a bleak picture, but it is not my intention to rub your nose in it.

The point is that this mechanism is wired from birth; it is the human condition, and unless it is exposed by inquiry and managed by the Yoga of the Three Energies, it will frustrate you until the day you die. Furthermore, the fact that it is hardwired means that you don't have to blame yourself and feel guilty about it. You should not draw the conclusion that you are a failure if your life is not working. This frustrating psychological mechanism is just what everyone has to work with when they appear here in a body.

The Solution

If dominant *rajas* and/or *tamas* or equal proportions of them don't solve the problem, the conclusion is obvious, since only one *guna* remains. If you subordinate *rajas* and *tamas* to *sattva*, everything will go smoothly because *sattva* supplies the steady alertness and dispassion required to pick up on the warning thoughts that come before the *rajas* energy is about to erupt. It gives you the clarity to evaluate the content of the thought and accept or dismiss it with reference to your highest value, the knowledge of who you are or, if you are a *sam-*

sari, with reference to a worldly goal. In this way *rajas* is denied the opportunity to mature into deluding emotions that will inevitably lead to *karmic* problems. A mind driven by emotions is not conducive to happiness. A knowledge-based mind easily creates a successful life.

How Do the Gunas Bind?

A. **They bind by attachment to results.** *Jivas,* created by *rajas,* are doers by nature. They do actions to enjoy the results. They need results for enjoyment because they don't enjoy themselves. How could they? They are endlessly dissatisfied because they feel incomplete. When they get what they want, they momentarily feel good. They conclude that the object contains joy and they become attached to it.

B. **They bind by attachment to relative knowledge.** Relative knowledge is knowledge of objects. The world is objects, and objects are nothing but knowledge pre-existing in the mind of *Isvara,* the Creator.

Objects behave according to certain laws. If they were not under the control of the laws, we would not get out of bed in the morning, because the inviolable connection between an action and a result would not be operational. Why would I brush my teeth if the cosmic program changed its mind one fine day and subsequently brushing led to tooth decay? Yes, teeth decay for other reasons, but brushing is not one of them. To successfully gain objects *jivas* need to know the rules that control them. For instance, a butcher must have knowledge of the anatomy of a cow or he cannot do his job. A teacher needs knowledge to teach. A salesman needs knowledge of psychology or he can't sell.

C. **They bind by attachment to thoughts and emotions.** Each *guna* produces signature thoughts and emotions. You bought a forty-acre parcel on the side of a mountain abutting public land where no one else could build and destroy your view. It was as if you owned the whole mountain. You got an architect to make the plans for your dream house and construction began. One day you walked to the back of the property and discovered a group of unsavory people squatting in the woods just beyond your property line. The pristine landscape was littered with trash and smelled abominably. The very thought of them made you furious, and you asked them to leave, but they wouldn't. They laughed at you first, then went about their business as if you didn't exist. They had every right to be there – it was public land after all and they were – well – the public. What could you do?

The *gunas* are unconscious forces sitting just beyond the boundary of your primary instrument going about their business irrespective of your wishes. They create your thoughts and bind you to them. If you want to control your destiny, you need to wrest control of your thought process. If you leave it to the *gunas* anything can happen.

Four Types of Thinking

Understanding the following four types of thinking are necessary before you begin to work on yourself.

A. **Impulsive involuntary thinking:** *Maya* is very subtle, complex and difficult to understand. We are looking at it from the point of view of the three *gunas*, the basic energies that create, maintain and destroy all the experiences that take place in the field of existence. In addition to producing the three *gunas*, each of which has an upside and a downside, *Maya* creates a big problem with its signature power, *viparaya*. *Viparaya* is a very important word, so please commit it to memory. It means "reversal."

What does it reverse? It disastrously reverses the basic relationship between the Self, the subject, and the objects the Self experiences. It so happens that the *jiva*, the doer/enjoyer entity, is an object known to the Self. But the doer/enjoyer thinks it is the subject and everything else is an object! If it hears of the Self, it understands the Self to be another object, and if it has spiritual *vasanas*, it will be inclined to pursue it as an object, when in fact it is the essence of the doer/enjoyer, a futile pursuit supported by most modern spiritual teachers. The seeker is informed that he or she must experience the Self and that the teacher's methods will provide such an experience, when in fact the seeker is, was and ever will be experiencing the Self because the Self is all there is.

With the help of Vedanta, an enlightened person transcends the *gunas*, reverses the reversal and returns the subject and the objects to their natural order.

When the reversal takes place, a secondary reversal takes place in the *jiva's* equipment: the natural relationship between the emotions and the intellect is also reversed. The intellect of mature, worldly and enlightened people is the boss, and the emotions take orders from it. But if you have been under the spell of *Maya*, meaning the *gunas*, for a very long time, you have never matured and your emotions call the shots. You "think" with your feelings.

Feelings are not something that should do your thinking, because they keep you from thinking. They are just unconscious reactions to events based on your likes and dislikes, your *vasanas*. Previously a certain situation caused anger, which may or may not have been justified, but the next time a similar situation arises you become angry even though anger is totally inappropriate.

If someone points out the fact that you are angry, the extent of your thinking usually involves denying you are angry in an angry voice and providing copious reasons why anger is the right call. Obviously, impulsive thinking is not the way to go if you want to control your destiny.

Vedanta has no quarrel with feelings and emotions. You are always feeling something. And if you are happy as your emotions push you around, fine. Unfortunately, nobody enjoys negative emotions. Negative emotions are generated by negative thoughts – thoughts that are not in harmony with the nature of reality – so glamorizing and romanticizing your feelings just keeps you from choosing the thoughts that produce enjoyable feelings.

B. **Mechanical, automatic thinking:** At least impulsive thinking, painful as it may be, makes you imagine that you are alive, which is probably better than mechanical thinking, which more or less reminds you that you are virtually dead. Most worldly people are little better than robots, sleepwalking through life, owing to the fact that they are completely controlled by their *vasanas*. Once you have your routines, the burden of conscious thought is lifted and, well, you do what you do, but then so does your wristwatch. Unfortunately, mechanical thinking, haven that it is for the unimaginative, doesn't work that well, because the *dharma* field presents situations that require responses that are different from your stock replies. If you fail to respond appropriately, you can count on a dose of pain.

Projection and Denial

Projection and denial aren't really "thinking" as we understand the word, because you are usually aware of your thoughts. These twin forces come from the deepest level of *Maya* and cause endless suffering. Projection is *rajas*. Projection means that ignorance puts a thought in your mind that may or may not correspond to the reality of a given situation, and *tamas* makes you think that the thought is the reality of the situation. It denies you access to the source, so you think it is true because it is "your" thought and that reality will benefit from it, which may or may not be true. In other words, you can't tell the difference between what you think and what is going on in the world around.

Do thoughts actually belong to you? They do, but they don't. They don't, because they are generated unconsciously by habit, but since no one but you identifies with them, they become "your" thoughts.

You could also argue that "you" created the *vasanas* because *vasanas* don't exist without actions and "you" did the actions, but did "you" do them or did the *gunas*, which you didn't create, cause the thoughts and the actions?

Other conscious beings who are the beneficiaries of your thoughts are unaware that *avidya* is the source, and that ignorance is hard at work in their subconscious minds projecting beliefs and opinions which they think are real, so they can't understand what you mean and you can't understand what they mean. This causes conflict, usually arguments which lead to argumentation tendencies, which do not bode well for happiness.

Projection also means that you think the object that you're experiencing, another person, for instance, caused the thought, but is that true? For example, you are riding in a car, and your normally voluble companion is quiet, for no other reason than that she has nothing to say. But you believe that her silence is a comment on your driving, which hasn't been particularly spectacular, to be sure; you nearly collided with a car a few blocks back because your cell phone rang and you were fumbling in your purse to retrieve it, but you didn't think it was your fault, because you answer your phone all the time when you are driving and nothing happens, so you blame the other driver. Blame is the poster child for projection.

Anyway, as you pass a familiar landmark your companion says, "We're almost there, we just passed Pizza Hut," which you did. You were paying attention to the road after the close call, so you didn't see it, and because your mind was distracted by the irritation caused by the other driver who had just "carelessly jeopardized your life," to use your own words, you snapped at your companion, "That wasn't Pizza Hut. It's coming up!"

Your companion, who was quiet and paying attention to the scenery, calmly said, "No, that was Pizza Hut," because it was. No projection, just an observable fact. This made you even angrier, so you said, "You always contradict me!," which wasn't true. It was just her statement of fact that interfered with your belief that the thought in your mind was real. Game on.

To wrap up this sad story, you honestly believed that your companion secretly thinks you are a bad driver, which does your self-esteem no good. You honestly believed that the close call was the other guy's fault and you sincerely believed that your companion was wrong about the location of that particular Pizza Hut. Nothing can convince you otherwise, because you "experienced" reality that way. You may have experienced reality that way, but you didn't experience reality as it was unless reality for you is your thoughts.

More examples: you blame America for all the trouble in the world. If it wasn't for America the world would be fine. The fact is that nobody ever saw an America. America is a projection, a thought. Many Americans think that America is the world's savior. Who is right, the yeasayers or the naysayers? Was America "America" before it was inhabited by Europeans? The native Indians didn't think so. You may have been to California, but did you find any object anywhere that had "California" written on it, apart from a tee-shirt in San Francisco that obviously is only a collection of cotton threads? You saw buildings and people, but that's all you see anywhere on the earth. America and California are projections, and a projection can be anything you want it to be. But what you want and reality are two different things. It helps to know the difference.

You Think the Distortion Is Reality

What isn't a projection? Everything you think and feel – your experience – is an abstraction, a stream of thoughts – memories, actually garnered from the past and superimposed on reality. There is a material transactional reality connected to your body that seems to be away from you, but you never jump out of your body to experience a tree, for example. If there is no thought in your mind and you open your eyes in the presence of a tree, you will have a tree-thought. That thought is not a projection. It had nothing to do with you. It is a thought that is true to the object. The tree-thought just is. It doesn't mean anything. It isn't a "nice" tree or an "ugly" tree. It is just something that is actually there, not something that you're putting there. You can argue that your thoughts are actually there too and you would be right, but you don't have the same relationship to them that you have to a tree. They are more than just "there." They imply something.

What they "mean" is added to them by *rajas, Maya's* projecting power, and *Maya's* veiling power keeps you from understanding that the pure perception of reality is actually distorted by your thinking. You think the distortion is reality.

Projection causes suffering because reality exists independently of your projections. So when reality demands a response, and you respond from your projections, you are asking for emotional problems because every situation is new and demands that you think on your feet. It needs what it needs, not necessarily what you think is good for it. If you don't give it what it wants, it will anger you or depress you. Thinking what happened caused your emotions is just another projection. Reality does not have it in for you. It just doesn't care what you think and feel. It is only friendly to grown-ups. We will presently see how to get out of this problem.

In any case, life is unfulfilling and you are an unfulfilled – dare I say boring? – person if your thinking is purely mechanical. However, life is good when you are in control of your thoughts and exceptionally wonderful when you think spontaneously.

C. **Deliberate thinking:** The notion in the spiritual world that the mind needs to be destroyed or transcended if you want to be happy is caused by the belief that the mind is only capable of impulsive and mechanical thinking, both of which are suffering. Your thoughts seem to be etched in stone because they relentlessly occupy your mind whether you want them or not. The same thoughts torture you ad nauseam. You just want to shut them off. The perennial attraction to drugs, alcohol and other pastimes lies in their ability to give relief from the tyranny of your thoughts. I once asked a woman why she kept a messy house, and without a trace of irony, she replied, "Because my mother did." There is absolutely no reason why her house should be messy except for the thought that she developed as a result of observing her mother's housekeeping skills. Actually, her messy house was a bother, and she would have been a lot happier if she was able to find things when she wanted them.

Your Thoughts Are Not Etched in Granite

You will be happy to hear this news: your thoughts are not etched in granite. You can think deliberately. This book is not writing itself. I am deliberately selecting thoughts and arranging them in a logical sequence because thinking these thoughts will transform your life. I'm not selecting every thought that passes through my mind, only those that are relevant to the topic, and I often change a thought minutes or weeks after I have written it if it is off-topic. If you have an emotional problem, you can remove it quickly if you take your mind off the emotion, find the thought that is creating it and choose a replacement thought that produces a more helpful emotion. Vedanta is a big Christmas package of replacement thoughts that will totally transform your life and set you free.

D. **Spontaneous thinking:** Those who transcend the *gunas* think spontaneously. To get there, you need to know what reality is and deliberately think thoughts that correspond to reality. This is where Vedanta is useful. It teaches you what reality is. When you understand what it is, you can very clearly see which of your thoughts are true and which are projections. If you know what a projection is, you will not be inclined to express it, because projections cause pain and create bad *karma*. Vedanta is deliberate thinking; it requires effort, unlike emotional and mechanical thinking. This is why it is not popular. This book will not become a bestseller, even though it contains the secret to success.

People are extremely lazy when it comes to disciplining their minds, particularly the spiritual crowd which threw the intellectual baby out with the bathwater a long time ago. They just want to feel good, not realizing that feelings are intimately bound up with thoughts. If you think, "I'm a useless worm," you are not going to feel wonderful. It you think, "I am the light of lights," you will feel great, assuming you understand what it means. Actually, the spiritual world is fascinated with certain kinds of thoughts, *mantras*, for instance. *Mantras* are just cleverly designed thoughts. They have an experiential component created by the artful arrangement of pleasing sounds, and they have an intellectual component, a particular meaning which needs to be taught and then contemplated. The experiential component calms the mind and produces bliss. The knowledge component gives insight into the nature of reality. But teasing the meaning out of the *mantra* and applying it to the mind on a moment-to-moment basis is hard work. Better to just get into a trance and bliss out.

Spontaneous thinking is appropriate to every situation and it is effortless. It takes a lot of disciplined thinking to get to this point, but it is totally worth it. It feels as if you aren't thinking, which you aren't! Reality in the form of the *dharma* field is thinking through you. The thoughts just naturally arise and pass through your mind without disturbing you. There is no resistance (*rajas*) or attachment (*tamas*) to them, because the *rajasic* doer has been neutralized by self-knowledge, and only the *sattvic* enjoyer remains. The thoughts are appropriate, interesting, humorous, ironical and truthful, and they always have a beneficial effect on others. They are *guna*-free in the sense that they are not motivated by a desire to get something or to fix something.

Two *Guna*-Based Personality Types

Because there is basically no complete scripture-based teaching in the modern spiritual world except for Vedanta, many people are attracted to astrology and the enneagram for knowledge of their subtle-body selves. They tend to be dismissive of the *guna* analysis because they think it is too simple; they feel that humans are much more complex and deserve a lot more attention. They don't realize that the *guna* model encompasses as much complexity as is humanly possible because the human organism is made up of many interconnected layers – we call them the Five Sheaths – and each sheath is made up of many parts. Furthermore, the *guna* configuration of one part can be different from the *guna* configuration of any other part.

For instance, the subtle body has four basic components, and each of those components has many components. There are five perceptive senses, five active senses, five physiological functions, mind – which has several functions – intellect, ego and the bliss sheath. Any one of those or its subcomponents can be dominated by a particular *guna* or a particular combination of *gunas*! You want complexity? We have it, not to mention we throw in self-knowledge and knowledge of the cosmos. And more to the point, if you understand the basic action of all the *gunas*, you can apply this knowledge to any aspect of yourself and transform it accordingly.

Because there are three *gunas*, and *rajas* and *tamas* are inseparable, there are only two basic personality types, both of which can be further subdivided.

When we speak about personality types in Vedanta, we are referring to your primary instrument: the mind and its tendencies. In this discussion *sattva*, *rajas* and *tamas* are not *gunas* but the fundamental orientation of the mind, your overarching attitude toward life: your body, wealth, people, spirituality, food, work, recreation, charity – anything at all. All these affect your relationship to *Isvara*, the conscious Creator of life, which needs to be a healthy relationship if you want to grow. Your personality is the way you think, your beliefs, value structure and priorities. The purpose of speaking in terms of personalities is not to give you an identity but to encourage you to develop *sattva*.

1. Classy, High-Minded People

Predominant *sattva* produces refined, considerate, mature people whose lives are guided by *dharma*. This category can be further divided into three: first, extremely intelligent, *sattvic*, high-minded people, sometimes called celestials, who are markedly disinterested in the world and tend to have excellent *karma*, which consistently generates fortuitous circumstances; they tend to be viewed by society as disassociated, incompetent, goofy malcontents, but are far from it. Second, reasonably satisfied, ethical, secular humanists with charitable instincts, but few spiritual inclinations and little or no value for liberation; and finally, evolved, self-aware people with varying degrees of desire for freedom.

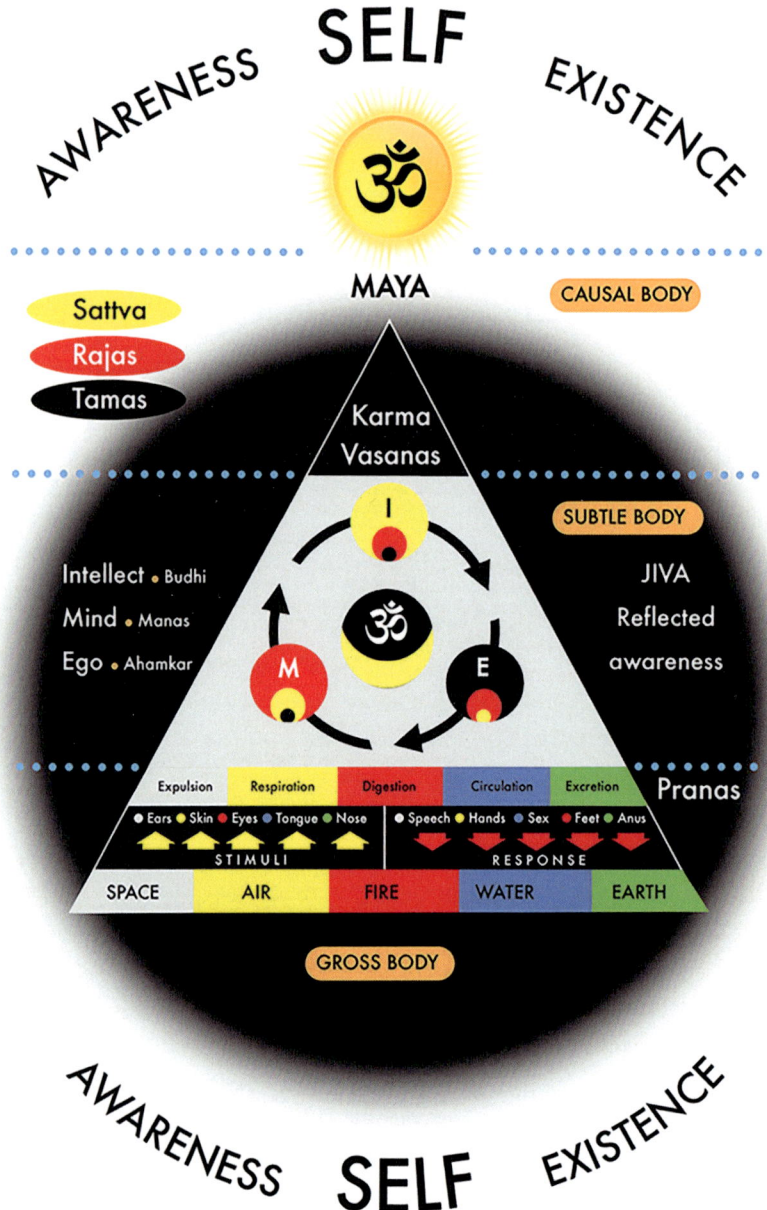

2. Self-Centered People

Rajas/tamas produces unrefined, impulsive, extroverted, mechanically-thinking people who are not necessarily unaware of *dharma* but whose lives are dictated by their desires and fears, likes and dislikes. This category can be further divided into highly self-centered people lacking esthetic or spiritual tendencies who dissipate their time and prodigious energy pursuing convenient, frivolous, sensuous, expedient things. Because the end is more important than the means, they inadvertently harm themselves and are unaware of the harm they do to others.

These people are not self-aware and do not understand their emotions. They have no interest in spirituality and favor fundamentalist religions. They don't believe in free will, as their social conditioning, which inoculates them from criticism from non-tribal members, is extremely rigid. They don't trust education, are fiercely anti-intellectual and are susceptible to propaganda. They fear change.

The second subcategory are sociopaths and psychopaths. Most human interactions are based on right (*dharma*) and wrong (*adharma*), the understanding that proper behavior leads to desirable results and that improper behavior leads to undesirable results. We say that if you accept the law of right and wrong, then you need to also accept an ordainer of the law, let's call it God, who delivers the results of actions. Sociopaths and psychopaths disagree; they say there is no ethical basis for action and that lust creates the world.

Predominate *tamas*, subordinate *rajas* and virtually no *sattva* produces godless, predatory, cruel, violent, *tamasic* people who take pleasure in harming others. They present an ever-present danger to the *dharma* field and need to be quarantined. The worst of the worst liberally stock the prisons, but many roam society looking for victims.

Sitting at the gates of hell – desire, anger and greed – they fancy themselves as masters of the universe, pursue power and wealth, and accumulate enemies they are eager to destroy. They believe that life is nothing more than the union of sperm and egg, so they have no concept of the moral order that brings about rebirth. Without a concept of right and wrong, everyone and everything is fair game. Because life, to quote Thomas Hobbes, is "nasty, brutish and short," they feel justified in grabbing as much as they can as quickly as they can before they die. These pea-brained people are even confused about trivial things; they can fly into a rage at the slightest provocation, real or imagined. Because the end justifies the means, they are capable of great cruelty and owing to grandiosity pursue desires that are impossible to fulfill.

You Are Not Your Personality

It may be news to you, but thank God you are not your personality. So it is important not to associate your Self with the *guna* dominating your subtle body at any moment. You are not *rajasic, tamasic* or *sattvic.* However, *Maya* will try to convince you that you are. It seems logical if you don't take the fact that you are identified with your subtle body into account. It's not really logical, however, because you don't experience yourself as three different people; you are just one simple conscious being. So if you say that you are *tamasic* in the morning when you get up, what happens to you when *rajas* or *sattva* dominates the subtle body? You aren't *tamasic* anymore. You are someone else, which is not possible.

Chapter V
The Gunas *and* Goals

IF YOU WANT something from life – and who doesn't? – then your *gunas* should match your goals. It is the same for a materialist chasing *samsaric* ends or an inquirer committed to freedom from *samsara* altogether. Obviously, you are influenced by all three because there are only three, but the right *guna* needs to manifest at the right time if you want to be successful. Remember, the world from which you are begging results is a great *guna* time clock that waits for no man.

If the pain of *rajas* makes you offer your action to the world too early or *tamas* causes you to wait too long, the chances of a favorable result are nil. Furthermore, the relationship between your *gunas* should be such that they maximize the chances of getting what you want. If you're running a marathon or creating a start-up, you need very little *tamas*, preferable none, although none is not an option. *Tamasic* people are completely non-competitive and accomplish very little in life. If you're trying to tease out the meaning of Vedantic *mantras*, you need mostly *sattva*.

The *guna* brief for committed self-inquirers is etched in granite. You use *rajas* to remove unnecessary *tamas* and sublimate *rajas* into *sattva* by changing the number and nature of your activities, keeping just enough *rajas* to do what needs to be done, no more. *Rajas* should be your friend. If you don't get it under control, it is your worst enemy. In case you still have any doubts about it, *rajas* is desire. It definitely has its upside – what is accomplished without desire? – but it is a serious enough problem that the Buddha categorically stated that it was the sole cause of suffering. It is probably more accurate to point out that desire is suffering, because you always have everything you need.

The Nature of the *Gunas*

A. *Sattvaguna* is the revealing power. The word "*sattva*" comes from the word "*sat*." *Sat* is pure existence/consciousness.

It is not physical light, which comes later when the fire element evolves, but it is eternal unborn awareness/consciousness because of which objects are known. As you will recall, *sattva* appears as the "mirror of matter" at the very beginning of Creation. It is called a mirror because it reflects awareness brightly and is the basis of the subtle body, the knowing instrument. So its basic function is to reveal objects. When it is the predominant *guna*, the *jiva* is alert and concentrated. *Sattva* allows it to dispassionately investigate situations and live an efficient, knowledge-based life. It is a peaceful, inspiring, kindly, happy energy.

B. **Rajoguna** is the projecting power that sets the cosmos in motion. It shatters the pure *sattva* into innumerable conscious entities and creates the dynamic forces operating in the material world: thermodynamics, electricity, nuclear fusion, etc. One of the meanings of *rajas* is "dust." *Rajas* stirs up a cloud of fine, dusty particles when it shatters the pure mirror of matter and mixes with *tamas,* which creates confusion and suffering for human *jivas.* It also creates subjective experience – thoughts, feelings, emotions, dreams, fantasies, desires, fears, etc. – out of subtle matter. It is a spiking, driving, dancing, aggressive, demanding, fickle energy. If it is intense, its powerful vibrations motivate great undertakings. If your desire for liberation, the greatest human undertaking, is not strong, you will not succeed. Unfortunately, its vibrations also create a distorted screen of thoughts and emotions that prevent accurate perception and careful analysis. Along with its kissing cousin *tamas,* it is responsible for erroneous knowledge.

C. **Tamoguna** is the concealing power called *avarana shakti. Avarana* is the Sanskrit word for "cloud." It is a particular kind of thought that envelops the subtle body in darkness and makes sleep possible. It is absolutely essential for a healthy life. When it lingers in the mind on waking or appears as a result of too much activity, it creates confusion and, like *rajas,* is responsible for erroneous knowledge.

The *Gunas* and the Primary Instrument ~ Assimilation of Experience and Knowledge

....
"Assimilation is the interpretation of experience."
....

Experience is an unbroken series of inner and outer events, and the *jiva's* reaction or response to them. The reaction of animals to experience is totally programmed. Humans have an advantage because they have the power to think.

They can study their experience, extract knowledge from it and change it, freeing themselves to some degree from their programming. Spiritual growth comes about through the proper assimilation of experience. Just as partially digested food inhibits the efficient functioning of the body, partially or improperly assimilated experience compromises the development of the subtle body.

Because awareness illumines the body-mind entity, your body is propelled through life according to its *karma*. As long as the meaning of its experiences is unknown to it, the person is little more than an animal and cannot fulfill its ultimate destiny.

Like an animal, a human infant unknowingly lives out its subconscious tendencies. It grows physically, but it does not evolve. It has no control over the direction of its life, because it has insufficient experience and knowledge to make informed choices. Once its intellect develops and it assimilates certain values, it can evaluate its experiences and begin to evolve.

The longer an experience remains unassimilated, the more problems it causes. Let us say that your father was an alcoholic and abused your mother so that she fell into a lifelong depression and was unable to raise you and your siblings properly. Because you were the eldest, you ended up parenting your younger brothers and sisters. You did it because you had no choice. You developed a deep resentment toward your father for robbing you of your childhood and a deep sympathy for your poor victimized mother. In reality, she was not blameless, because she never stood up to her husband; she actually enabled his alcoholism in subtle ways.

Nonetheless, you projected her as a martyr and loved her for it. Your father died, but your hatred lived on. You believed a grave injustice had been done and it colored your feelings toward men in general. One day a nice man wanted to marry you, and in the excitement of first love you agreed, but as time went on certain things your husband said or did reminded you of your father, which brought up old feelings of resentment and rage. You began to pick quarrels with him for no reason. Your fears slowly got the best of you and you incorrectly imagined that these small personality traits he shared with your father – a certain inflection in his voice when he was stressed, for example – revealed a selfish and abusive nature. You accused him of changing and said he did not really love you, which was not true. Your relationship deteriorated and your children started to become neurotic. You confided in one of your divorced women friends, who came from a similar background and was holding a grudge against her ex. She showed so much concern for your plight that you fell in love with her, left your husband, abandoned your children and became gay. But after a while your new identity did not work, because you loved her for the wrong reason: she was not a man.

Had your mother been the abuser, you may have hated women and loved men. We can make this story go on and on for fifty years or more, each tragic event unfolding out of the preceding event like clockwork until it becomes impossible to work back to the beginning, discover the reason for the suffering and heal the wound.

Experience does not interpret or assimilate itself. The intellect interprets experience. It sits behind the mind and evaluates what happens. If experience conforms to the ego's desire, it gives the thumbs-up and positive feelings arise. If life delivers experience contrary to its desire, it gives the thumbs-down and negative feelings arise. How it interprets experience depends on acquired knowledge and ignorance plus three factors that are normally beyond its control. Two factors inhibit its ability to discriminate and one facilitates it. The factors are *rajas, tamas* and *sattva. Rajas* and *tamas* tend to inhibit assimilation, and *sattva* facilitates it.

RAJAS AND ASSIMILATION

How does *rajas* affect the assimilation of experience? Whether the goals are worldly or spiritual, and whether or not they are realized, the *rajasic* intellect is not concerned with the truth of experience, only with how a particular experience relates to the fulfillment of the ego's desires.

Rajas is always a source of frustration because everything gained is inevitably lost. An object gained causes attachment, and an object lost produces grief, neither of which is conducive to happiness.

Rather than accept the impermanence of life as a fact and be satisfied with what is, *rajas* causes the ego to continually seek fulfillment in new experiences.

Even though the individual knows better, *rajas* can cause such a lack of discrimination that you consistently repeat actions that produce suffering. It often generates so many actions in such a short time that the intellect can never determine which action was responsible for a given result, thus preventing it from learning from its experiences.

When a pleasurable experience ends, *rajas* causes disappointment because the ego wants the pleasure to continue, even though the intellect knows that pleasure is fleeting. If an experience is mediocre, it wants it to be better. If it is bad, it should end instantly and not happen again. If experience repeats itself over and over, as it does owing to conditioning, *rajas* causes boredom and produces a strong desire for variety. "More-better-different" is its holy *mantra*. It produces an endlessly active, time-constrained life of frustrating loose ends.

No matter how much is accomplished, the to-do list never shrinks. *Rajas* is a closet, garage, basement and attic overflowing with a confusing assortment of neglected and unused objects. It is a late tax return, a forgotten appointment, an unreturned call, a frantic search for one's keys. *Rajas'* aggressive, extroverted forays into *samsara* are inevitably accompanied by fatigue and insomnia.

When I was young, my father, who was wise in many ways, used to say, "You can't win." At the time I did not understand what he meant, but a life well spent and the teachings of Vedanta made it clear: life is a zero-sum game, an eternal war within oneself in which neither side prevails for long. For example, when *tamas* appears in a person whose predominant *guna* is *rajas*, a painful experience is inevitable.

You have many things on your to-do list, but your mind is so dull that every action becomes painful. You are wired but tired. It is not fun. And conversely when you need to indulge your *tamas* and sleep, your mind is too busy. So you suffer. How did you get into this unenviable position? You repressed the sleep-thought because you were so wrapped up in the world that you didn't like the idea of wasting time. The sleep-thought is a message from *Isvara*, an early-warning beeper that informs you that the time is right to slow down and enter the arms of Morpheus. Ignore it at your peril.

Proper assimilation takes place only when the mind is alert and present. Therefore when *rajas* dominates the subtle body the innate wisdom of the Self, much less common-sense knowledge, is not available to help the intellect accurately determine what is happening and resolve doubts.

Resolved experience leaves attention fully present so that it is able to meet the next experience without prejudice. Because life is an unending procession of experiences in this pressurized age, it is important to lay each experience to rest as quickly as possible, preferably as it ends. When you are so *rajasic* that your mind is totally wrapped up in dealing with an endless succession of trivial daily desires, you are too busy to look at your issues, so they remain in the background and cause suffering.

Unresolved experience subliminally drains attention. Difficulty focusing on what needs to be done and avoidance of what should or should not be done are signs that the mind is excessively *rajasic*. As unresolved experience accumulates, the individual suffers existential constipation and feels overwhelmed, stressed and unable to keep up. Growth rarely comes through the easy attainment of desires, but an extroverted person is also denied the growth-enhancing benefits produced by the assimilation of unwanted experiences.

TAMAS AND ASSIMILATION

Tamas, the veiling power, inhibits the assimilation of experience as efficiently as *rajas*, but for different reasons. Under its influence the subtle body, though seemingly quiet, is actually dull. Efficient evaluation of experience requires mental clarity, but when a torpid veil covers the subtle body, perception is muddied and assimilation is compromised. When the intellect is dull, it has difficulty connecting the results of its actions with the thoughts motivating them, causing uncertainty with respect to what should or should not be done. When the subtle body is predominately dull, you are negotiating the ocean of *samsara* in a ship without a compass or a rudder. "Where should I go? What should I do? What's going on? I don't know. I do not want to know," are some signature thoughts.

A *tamasic* mind runs unthinkingly on conditioned patterns. Unlike *rajas*, it hates the new because it is forced to adjust. Because creative thinking takes so much energy, the *tamasic* mind does not value inquiry. Therefore it cannot gain control of events and is forced to continually revisit negative situations. Consequently *tamas* is responsible for the feelings of helplessness that cause deep and lasting depressions.

Tamas solves problems by denying them. When unwanted *karma* happens, it teams up with *rajas* to lay the blame elsewhere. The undigested experiential backlog brought on by a *tamasic* mind causes the ego to dither and procrastinate. If you have a *rajasic* lifestyle and feel constantly exhausted, know that *rajas* is causing *tamas*. When *tamas* is particularly heavy, even small daily duties like brushing teeth, combing hair or taking out the garbage seem like gargantuan undertakings. Neglect is *tamasic* and is responsible in large part for the rampant emotional dysfunction seen in materialistic societies.

Parents become so caught up in their own lives that children are neglected. Unloved children quickly develop low self-esteem and are unable to properly fulfill their roles in society.

Sattva and Assimilation

There are no experiential qualifications for liberation, only the right *guna* balance. If the mind is predominately *sattvic* it can assimilate information carefully and quickly lay experiences to rest. A persistent "issue" means that you have an assimilation problem and inquiry will be difficult.

I have a friend who was adopted. His mother gave him up to a good family for adoption when he was very young. He was loved and given all the advantages. But when he was told he was adopted, he developed a terrible complex and was incapable of assimilating the information properly. Had he been *sattvic* at that time, he would have realized that *Isvara* was great because an unfit mother had been eliminated and replaced with a good one. But his mind was *tamasic,* and he took it to mean he wasn't valuable. That idea stuck in his mind for more than fifty years. It ruined several marriages, and he did not find love until Vedanta came into his life, allowing him to evaluate his issue dispassionately.

When *rajas* dominates the mind, desire interprets experience. When *tamas* dominates, fear interprets experience. Both obscure the truth.

But when *sattva* dominates, truth interprets experience.

The physical body of every living being grows, maintains itself for some time, decays and dies. Without a *sattvic* spiritual infrastructure, a proper means of *guna*-knowledge and a teacher, the epiphany-born commitment to liberation that often sets one on the path follows the same pattern: a spurt of growth, an attempt to sustain it with willpower as the initial inspiration fades, a loss of interest and a return to the world. The secret to continual spiritual growth lies in continually increasing *sattva* with reference to *rajas* and *tamas.* If unnecessary *rajas* and *tamas* are not converted to *sattva,* inquiry becomes a stultifying ritual and growth stops.

THE TERRIBLE TWINS

Rajas and *tamas* are very useful energies, but only if they are subordinated to *sattva.* Dominant *rajas* and *tamas* create an extroverted, materialistic, cynical, selfishly negative, emotionally volatile, sunless personality, which may be useful for turning the wheels of commerce and industry, but is not a stellar combination for inquiry, which requires dominant *sattva.* The *Bhagavad Gita* labels individuals with dominant *rajas* and *tamas* "demonic." Together they blind instead of bind the mind to *dharma,* which, needless to say, puts you in conflict with the Creation, which in turn causes suffering.

A dramatic example of the incestuous relationship between *rajas* and *tamas* is manic depression, a disease which has run afoul of the political-correctness police of late and been relabeled "bipolar" to avoid offending the sensibilities of its sufferers. It is *rajas* and *tamas* on steroids. It is a good appellation for our discussion because it conveys the idea of duality very well; where you find one, you find the other.

Here is an everyday example of the symbiotic relationship between *rajas* and *tamas.* Your wife said, "Why didn't you turn off the light in the bathroom?" It is a fact that the light is on. The real issue is not waste, although she thinks it is, and even if it is for her, there is no reason why you can't "waste" a bit of electricity. Additionally, she was capable of turning the light off because she had just entered the bathroom. It is unlikely that idle curiosity prompted the question.

The statement implies that you did something "wrong." It is a blaming statement. Blame is a signature symptom of *rajas*, a violent sign of emotional discomfort. If she had been in a *sattvic* state, which inclines individuals to dispassion, she would have simply turned the light off and avoided conflict, knowing that people don't purposely leave the light shining when they leave a room. Or she could have politely mentioned it later in a non-judgmental way.

Comparison and Competition

Rajasic people also often need to feel that they are "right." What better issue than the waste of valuable resources to gain the moral high ground by diminishing your spouse? The need to gain the moral high ground is anchored in low self-esteem, which is not defined with reference to one's own failings, but with reference to the failings of others. If I am a self-aware inquirer, I know that the self-esteem issue has nothing to do with my relationship with others and I heal the issue on my own with reference to my stated goal, freedom from excessive *rajas* and *tamas*.

Comparing and competing are also signature *rajasic* energies. Comparison is a slippery slope. You see someone you admire and you think, "I want to be like her." You become jealous. Since you know that is not going to happen, you settle for less and think, "I want what she has," and the jealousy morphs into envy, a truly despicable emotion. Still frustrated, you think, "I will beat her. I will get her man." Rivalry. And finally, since none of the above emotions led to satisfaction, rivalry turns to hatred and malice: "I will destroy her."

Negative emotions expressed to others are usually unconscious attempts to manipulate them. The need to control others is also based on a feeling of low self-esteem. Anger and blame are part of an unconscious compensatory mechanism that makes the doer-ego momentarily feel powerful. In the bathroom light situation, the blamer wants to diminish her spouse with guilt (*tamas*). Without realizing it she is attempting to get rid of the *tamas* by transferring it because insecurity is uncomfortable. If her husband accepts the projection, she feels satisfied (*sattvic*). If not, her anger (*rajas*) increases and the argument heats up. As mentioned, her unconscious aim is to experience bliss when the anger is transferred.

But she actually has no control of her husband's *gunas*. It may create insincere compliance if he is *tamasic* because *tamoguna* inclines an individual to avoidance. A person under its spell may accept the projection, preferring the guilty feeling to extended conflict. *Tamasic* people often feel good feeling bad; it is essential to their identity because it generates sympathy, which makes them feel momentarily worthwhile (*sattva*). Or they may care, not in a thoughtful, dispassionate, *sattvic* manner, but in an ignorant, slothful way.

But if her husband is under the sway of *rajas*, he may very well be looking for a fight, as *rajasic* people tend to be contentious. So he may resist because, although we like to control, we don't like to be controlled (*sattva*). *Sattva* is love of freedom. In any case, neither the blamer nor the blamed can be blamed, because both are ignorant of who they are. Only understanding can solve this problem.

The simple non-violent statement "I forgot" should be sufficient to remove the tension because nobody thinks "I will forget" before they forget. Forgetting (*tamas*) is an unconscious act; willpower is not involved. This statement does not satisfy the blamer, because *rajasic* people tend to be overly sensitive. They attack so much they are used to being attacked, so they are always defensive. *Rajas* causes psychological pain. It is a violent, spiky, tearing, dualistic energy. It may cause your wife to assume that you left the light on consciously even though part of her – the Self – knows better. She sees your forgetting as a challenge (*rajas*) to her power when your words "I forgot" were simply an unemotional statement of fact (*sattva*). When you are challenged or in this case project a challenge where none exists, you feel insecure (*tamas*). She takes the projection (*rajas*) to be real because *tamas* is veiling her intellect. If you point out that she is projecting, she will angrily deny it. When you are insecure, your reaction is anybody's guess; you can take flight or you can attack. If you were *sattvic*, you wouldn't react at all.

In any case, if your predominant *guna* at the time, *rajas*, changes to *tamas* the moment you hear the words "why didn't you turn off the light!" you may retreat, in which case you will probably feel resentful (*rajas*) and look for an opportunity to even the score when your *rajas* returns. The need to even the score is *rajas* motivated by *sattva* because *sattva* reflects non-dual values, and justice is a non-dual value. It is not fair that your spouse accused you of deliberately leaving the light on in the bathroom, so you quietly vow revenge, a good example of the power of *sattva* to generate *rajas*.

If she picks up on your resistance, she may up the ante and insincerely ask, "Why did you forget?," which should be followed by an angry exclamation point, not a question mark. We have already established the fact that forgetting is involuntary, not volitional. When a thought is no longer needed, it drops out of the subtle body on its own. In this context "why did you forget?" is simply another blaming statement.

Any attempt to answer it at face value does not work, because it plays into the hands of the blamer. You are damned if you do and damned if you don't, a good example of the zero-sum nature of reality. *Rajasic* people love to feel aggrieved because it justifies action, to which they are hopelessly addicted. Desire is painful, anger more so. Blame is a convenient ploy to diffuse pain.

Rajasic people are obsessed with success and often find it elusive because they tend to act before it is appropriate or are completely disturbed emotionally when they act, which does not bode well for a favorable result, whereas *tamasic* people, famous for procrastination, act too late or not at all. *Rajas,* a gross, violent energy, pushes *sattva,* happiness, away. We are always striving for *sattva.* Unfortunately, *rajas* is so prized in achievement-oriented societies that it is accompanied by a strong sense of moral virtue, which in turn causes a value for action for its own sake, whether it is appropriate or not.

If an argument about something as trivial as a light in the bathroom which can lead to blows seems farcical, it is. However, both blamer and blamed are innocent victims. They don't want to argue, but they can't help it. Arguments are *guna*-generated. They are unconscious and are never about what they purport to be about. As with forgetting, you don't ever think, "I'll argue today." Arguments happen because my *guna*-driven values conflict with your *guna*-driven values when they are tweaked in certain situations. If you were my willing slave, we would never argue. Love does not mean that individuals should act out the desires of the people they love. Love should be big enough to let loved ones be themselves.

The solution? Become aware of the values associated with each *guna.* You can't see the *guna,* because it is hidden in the causal body, but you don't need to see it, because it inevitably appears in the subtle body as a value, a thought, and you can work on it from there.

Only two of the fourteen factors involved in a two-way transaction are known, your conscious mind and the conscious mind of the individual with whom you are speaking. The rest are unknown. Is it any wonder that conflict is virtually inevitable?

In the first place, you may not even know that there is another "you" behind the you that you think you are. This "you" is the Self: limitless, ordinary awareness. And if you do know the Self, is it known directly or indirectly? Is it known as an immediate, palpable, ever-present experience of yourself in the form of the "I" or do you know it indirectly as an object, something you experienced previously and are striving to experience? Or is it known merely as book knowledge or hearsay?

In every situation there are four basic factors: (1) the Self, which is uninvolved but shouldn't be ignored, (2) the macrocosmic unconscious mind, or *Isvara*, which is anything but unconscious, (3) the personal subconscious mind

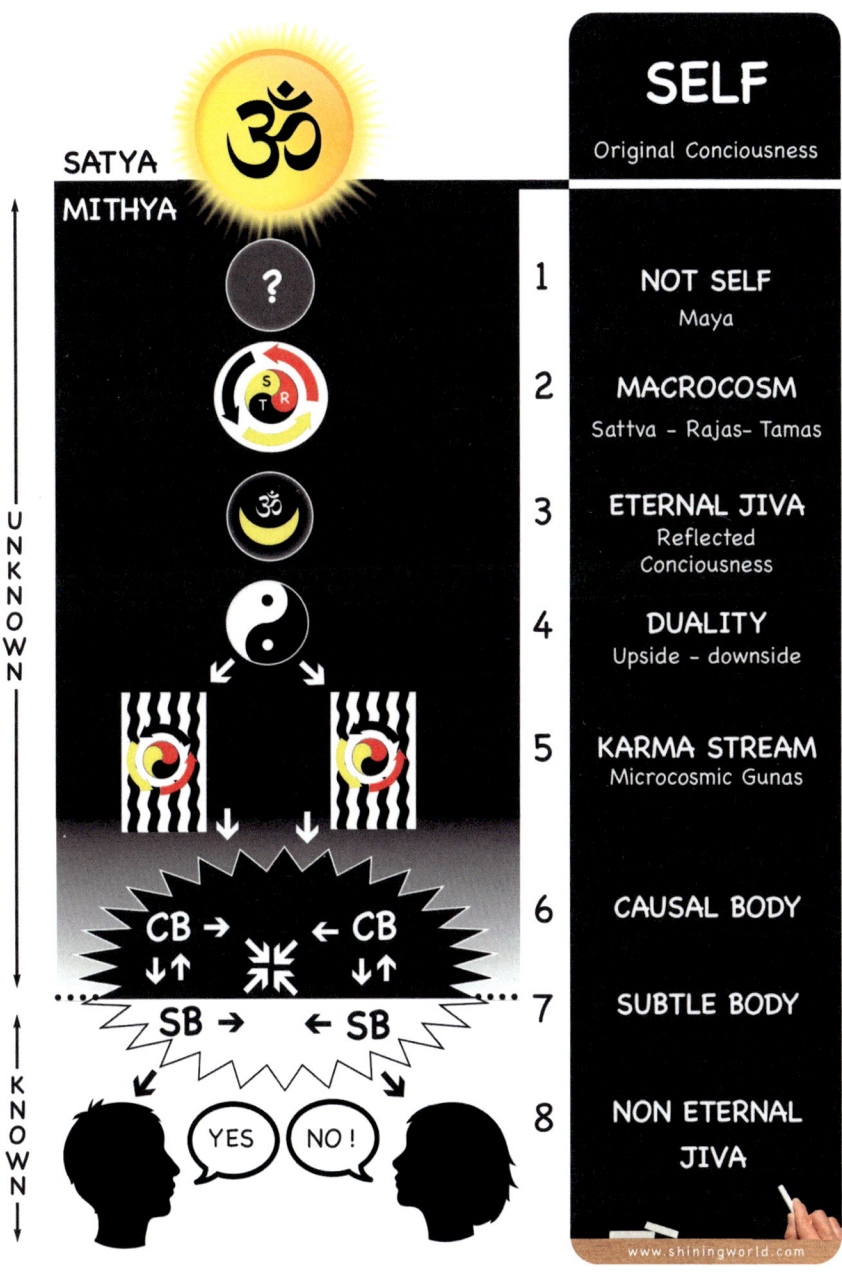

55

and (4) the personal subtle body, the individual's primary instrument of experience and knowledge.

Most of us only know what is appearing in the present on the level of the microcosmic subtle body. But what we experience is generated by our causal bodies, which are three ever-changing energies that keep our primary instruments in a state of constant flux. How could it be known directly, because like the Self, it is beyond sense experience? Nonetheless, it would be very helpful to understand it because everything we experience comes from it!

Moreover, your subconscious mind is directly influenced by the macrocosmic causal body, an even subtler level of reality that is also changing according to a different set of parameters, the needs of all the factors in the *dharma* field. Furthermore, your primary instrument is subject to free-will-induced particularities related to the dynamic situations that you confront every day. So that when you interact with others, you may be playing entirely different games with different hands while apparently sitting at the same table!

There is no solution on the level of the argument, because as they change, all the factors in the two orders of the apparent reality keep creating more problems.

If you expect life to be problem-free, you are deluded. Even liberation is liberation in spite of life. This is not to say that you can't create a flowing, happy life, but it is only possible when *rajas* and *tamas* have been thoroughly subordinated to *sattva*. *Rajas* and *tamas* confuse and particularize your vision, but *sattva* expands it, affording a panoramic view.

Two Orders of the Apparent Reality

The causal body, the unconscious mind, is the unknown order, and the subtle body, with which the *jiva* is identified, is the known. They are not integrated in unevolved people, so their lives are full of inner and outer conflict. Self-inquiry integrates them.

In any case, the solution is to kick-start inquiry the moment you find yourself in the conflict-producing (*rajas/tamas*) loop. To return to our example, the argument about wasting electricity, both may have the same value for conservation of material energy, but don't share a value for the conservation of emotional energy, which is essential for happiness.

Both have reasonable positions and both want relief, but both unwittingly feed the unconscious *rajas/tamas* syndrome. In addition to understanding the values associated with each *guna*, it's critical to recognize and respect the feeling of *rajas* and the feeling of *tamas*. If *rajas* or *tamas* is dominating your mind or another mind, the warning beeper should go on and you should immediately go into inquiry mode (*sattva*), i.e. bring the knowledge of *Isvara* and *jiva* to mind, and expose the workings of the projection/denial mechanism, which will put the conflict into perspective and neutralize it.

This peep into the factors behind everyday life notwithstanding, understanding the basics of human psychology does not require a degree in psychology or even an introductory course. Simple observation will suffice. The human being program is little more than its particular collection of fears and desires. These twin energies are locked in a passionate embrace because they are born of the same mother at the same time. That mother is *Maya*.

We will take up the downside of *sattva* later, but when these terrible twins team up, you have trouble on your hands. If you recall the discussion of the nature of *Maya* in Chapter III, there was no problem at stage one. Everything was copacetic. Pure, eternal, non-dual awareness illumined the pure *sattvic* mirror of matter, which contained the knowledge of everything – God dreaming the world, if you will.

THE BIRTH OF FEAR AND DESIRE

What could go wrong? Everything, it turns out. In the second stage, enter *rajas*, stage left. *Rajas* pollutes the *sattva* with *tamas* and then, like a spoiled baby, shatters it into *jiva* bits – the conscious beings – and scatters them throughout the cosmos where they are left to their own devices. This stage is called *avidya*. Roughly translated it means "ignorance," but it does not mean "stupid," although it includes stupidity. *Vidya* means "knowledge" or "science," and *avidya* means "unscientific" or "ignorance." Why is this stage the key to our discussion? Because this is where fear and desire are born. The *jiva*, bless its lovely *sattvic* nature, forgets who it is owing to the fact that the cloud of *tamas* hides it. Simultaneously it becomes a desire-ridden extrovert. Why? Because at the same time that the blissful fullness of its nature is being obscured by the *tamas*, *rajas* is projecting a fascinating, ever-changing array of juicy, sexy objects. See the problem? Our intrepid little *jivas* think that the emptiness they feel as a consequence of their loss of self-knowledge can be removed if only they can just capture some of those shiny baubles "out there." Game on. And the inevitable result? Life one, *jiva* nil.

Rajas and *Tamas* ~ Fear Is Desire, and Desire Is Fear

Fears (*tamas*) and desires (*rajas*) are the same, but different. A fear is a negative desire, and a desire is a positive fear. If you want something, there is a fear that you won't get it, and if you get it, there is a fear of losing it. Since the mind of a worldly person is nothing but things that it has and things it doesn't have, it is always bedeviled by fear and desire. Both are proxies for self-ignorance. So ignorance is not ignorance of things, it is ignorance of the fullness of our ever-free nature.

Objection: "So you say that fear and desire are the bedrock of *jiva's* personality, but isn't this a bit dramatic? Life is pretty good. I have it all: a job, a house in suburbia, a wife, kids and a nice car; what's to want? I'm not afraid."

Okay, but if you think about it, the fears are still there. "Your" job can always be made redundant at the hands of a heartless economy, "your" wife can always get fed up with your bad habits and run off with the guy next door, "your" kids can get messed up with sex and drugs, etc., etc.

Anyway, let's say you are pretty happy with the basics of your life – you got all the obligatory stuff that Mom and Pop and the TV wanted for you – pat on the back – but your desires are still there in a much more insidious form: your likes and dislikes, attractions and aversions.

What makes a successful materialistic life so wonderful is not the job and the glories of suburban culture, not at all. What makes it great is feeling that you are entitled to get as neurotic as you want at the hands of gratuitous likes and dislikes too numerous to mention. You have a modicum of security and now you deserve the luxuries. If there isn't a constitutional amendment guaranteeing unending luxuries, there should be.

Although you are loath to admit it, luxuries have become necessities and your attachment to them can leave you every bit as wanting as you were before you "had" them in the first place.

There is no spiritual growth if *rajas* and *tamas* dominate *sattva*, because you will always be at the mercy of the zero-sum nature of *samsara*, which is totally based on fears and desires, i.e. self-ignorance.

MORE SAD FACTS

You can't say that Vedanta teachers are clamoring for fame. If we were, we wouldn't be telling you all this. The feel-good modern non-dualists certainly don't happily regale you with such bad news. If they did they would have to get day jobs. Vedanta is brutal. It wants you to face the facts and man up. But if life is so wonderful, why are you looking for a way out? Honestly, when we get done with this analysis, you are probably going to wonder if *Isvara* isn't the Original Pervert, not the Original Consciousness.

The next thing you need to know about *rajas* and *tamas* is that the greater the *rajas* the stronger the *tamas*, resistance. For instance, you evolve a habit that takes care of a particular problem, a few drinks and a smoke after a hard day at the office to get rid of the *rajas*, which puts a rosy *sattvic* glow on everything and keeps you from snapping at your long-suffering wife and ignoring your needy kids when you get home. Fair enough, you deserve it. But it's not that simple. If you think back, your drinking and smoking probably started when you were an anxious *rajasic* teenager.

These habits momentarily calmed you down and made you feel better. Fast-forward twenty years: you've been managing your emotions this way ever since, but one fine day your doctor says your liver and lungs are packing it in – as they do. A new non-habit is required: you need to quit drinking while a handful of healthy cells remain. So why not "just say no," as the former First Lady, Nancy Reagan, used to plead from her bully pulpit as she ineffectually exhorted the druggie nation to abstinence.

What's the problem? Quitting shouldn't be difficult; you are not required to do anything. Not drinking is not doing, right? True, but the downside of those years of *rajas* comes home to roost the day you need to quit; you have become totally attached to the habit. This attachment is *tamas*, fear of losing something, never mind that it is a detrimental something. Our bad habits become our best friends. As a friend, who I was exhorting to clean up his life, replied, "It may be shit, James, but it's warm and it's mine."

If you had enough *sattva*, you would have been alert enough to understand that your parents were not trying to control you and that they had your best interests in mind when they advised you to go easy on the smokes and the booze. You might have nipped this habit in the bud and found less foolish ways to manage your emotions. When you are so attached to a bad habit – it can be anything, quarreling with your spouse, watching internet porn, eating junk food or checking your email fifty times a day, for instance – you will stick to it long past its sell-by date. You will keep right on doing what you are doing even though it delivers much more pain than pleasure. And, sad to say, if you fail to take the bull by the horns and kick it, you will end up squandering your few remaining mental and emotional resources in denial (*tamas*) and blame (*rajas*).

WIRED BUT TIRED: WORKING AGAINST YOURSELF

When you don't know who you are, you feel small, weak and inadequate. You believe this feeling adequately expresses who you are and you try to compensate by doing something. This feeling is a manifestation of the ignorance that produces *rajas,* which generates endless actions. If you are reasonably skillful and accomplish a few goals, you will start to feel powerful. Power is a dangerous aphrodisiac for a small mind. It will spur you on to bigger, but not necessarily better, things.

Ambition, one of *rajas'* signature symptoms, depending on how spiritually empty you feel, usually causes you to bite off more than you can chew, with predictably unfortunate results. So even though a deep sense of lack creates enormous desire, which generates a lot of transactions and a commensurate amount of stress, *tamas* grows and you start to tire, reducing your effectiveness.

If you had a reasonable amount of *sattva,* you would honor those feelings and build leisure into your life. At the very least you would make sure you slept properly. But you don't. You up the ante and do more, overriding the *tamas* until you are no longer alert enough to keep your thoughts in front of you where you can observe and manage them. When you get to this stage, the blinking red light should go on and you should cut back and take stock. If you don't, your discrimination will desert you and you will compromise everything you worked so hard to achieve.

You see the walls crumbling and you don't know what to do. Out of desperation you go to a psychic or a *guru* looking for a "spiritual" solution, a secret *mantra* perhaps. The spiritual solution is simple: OBEY YOUR *TAMAS!* But sleep is not a viable option. "I might miss out on something!" So you keep going. At this point life's tail is wagging life's dog, and the outcome is not a happy one.

The same psychology applies across the board to every human pursuit. Desire (*rajas*) for security (*sattva*) is born of fear (*tamas*) of insecurity (*rajas*).

Think obsession with gain and loss. Desire (*rajas*) for pleasure (*sattva*) is born of separation (*tamas*) and loneliness (*tamas*). Think relationships, drugs, alcohol and sex. Desire (*rajas*) for virtue (*sattva*) is born of ignorance of the Self (*tamas*) because you are the source of all virtue. Negative (*tamas*) moral judgments (*rajas*) are based on low self-esteem (*tamas*), the need to occupy the moral high ground. Desire (*rajas*) for beauty (*sattva*) is born of *tamas,* ignorance of the Self, the beauty that makes beauty beautiful.

To the degree that this tug of war between *rajas* and *tamas* dominates *sattva,* the zero-sum nature of *samsara* is either a mildly frustrating impediment to accomplishing one's goals or a seriously depressing obstacle. If you often feel "blocked," know that *rajas/tamas* is an issue that needs to be addressed.

Although there are many, from ill health to serious problems with society, one of the symptoms of this syndrome is irritability with small things because dispassion and accommodation, which are *sattvic* values, are not available to buffer your relationship with yourself and the world.

Dispassion is like a filter between the conscious mind, the subtle body, and the unconscious, the causal body. When it is suppressed, your primary instrument is exposed to whatever *rajasic* and *tamasic* energies are at play in the environment. If someone enters the room carrying bad energy, your mind will pick it up unconsciously and it will start to operate in you. You won't even know that it has happened and you will be surprised when a conflict erupts.

It's not so bad if you are angry with yourself, although it certainly isn't fun, but dominant *rajas/tamas* does not play well in social situations, because even trivial events can spark destructive emotional outbursts and ruin relationships, owing to *rajas'* famous projection mechanism, about which more will be said shortly. This is a real problem because you can almost never heal a relationship that has fallen victim to this syndrome. Breaking the rules of civil discourse is usually cause for immediate shunning and invokes shame (*tamas*) and pride (*rajas*). You are too ashamed to admit your transgression and too proud to mend fences.

In any case, excess *rajas* and *tamas* are problematic for another important reason: both distort perception, causing doubt and distrust. Although the world tends to glorify fear, it is not smart. It constricts the soul and stifles spontaneous, creative action.

Values Conflict ~ More Zero-Sum

Guna balance, equal parts of each *guna,* is often touted as the panacea for all that ails you, but equal parts of unequal things do not always work out well. For instance, a person with equal parts of *rajas* and *sattva* will be prone to conflict when *rajas'* demand for material solutions conflicts with *sattva's* demand for spiritual solutions. Someone with equal parts of *rajas* and *tamas* will experience conflict too. Fear (*tamas*) will cause you to second-guess and dither when *rajas* cooks up a plan of action that may save your bacon.

A person endowed with equal parts of *sattva* and *tamas* can easily become conflicted because *sattvic* and *tamasic* values are quite different. For instance, if you are spiritually-oriented, physically beautiful and ethical (*sattva*), with a desire (*rajas*) for security (*tamas*), and a wealthy, *rajasic* person is attracted to you, you may be tempted to barter your beauty for security, which creates conflict. What value is most important? *Sattva* inclines the mind to patience, honesty and integrity, whereas *rajas* pressures the mind for easy, often morally questionable solutions.

Do You Care What People Think?

Insecurity (*tamas*), the need to know where you fit in the pecking order, causes *rajas*, competition and comparison. You want to fit in and get what you want, so you care what people think. If you care what people think, you will tend to project an image that casts you in a favorable light. You will carefully control your physical appearance, your environment and your behavior. But this *rajasic* tendency contradicts your *sattvic* opinion of yourself as a spontaneous, natural human being. You hate (*rajas*) the idea that you are superficial and controlling, so to preserve your sense of integrity you lie to yourself and cook up fancy spiritual justifications for your superficiality. But you can't hide from yourself, so there is always a sense of inauthenticity when the *gunas* are in conflict.

Chapter VI
Karma Yoga

THE LOGIC OF the first five chapters is intended to convince you that Vedanta understands the cause of suffering and that there is a solution. It is shamelessly designed to appeal to your self-interest, inspire you to exercise your free will, roll up your spiritual sleeves and get to work, assuming you are serious about experiencing the freedom that is tantamount to non-dual love.

The immature, self-centered inner child needs to develop an objective view of itself and the world, and *karma yoga* is a straightforward, no-nonsense solution.

You needn't lavish money on a therapist or waste your weekends on silent retreats. You don't need to get a *guru* or run off to India to get enlightened. You can stay right where you are and convert everyday life into a powerful spiritual practice. And since you accrued your *karma* under your given name, it is a good idea to reduce it under the aegis of a different and provisional identity – *karma yogi.* We're not suggesting that you cook up a spiritual name, not at all, only that you think of yourself as a *karma yogi,* an identity that makes you objective toward yourself and a friend of the world, and an identity that obligates you to follow the program.

Before you set out to fix a problem, it is wise to gather information. Unfortunately, when you are suffering you tend to plunge into the shark-infested spiritual waters to quench the raging flames of *samsara* without checking to see what lies below the surface. If you do, you are in danger of hitting your head on the rocks, i.e. following personal, epiphany-based, so-called teachings, which are often little more than ill-considered opinions purveyed by a raft of unqualified, unpurified, ambitious, often sharky do-gooders out to save your sorry soul. No one else can save you. You need a common-sense, scripture-based, time-tested teaching that puts you in the driver's seat.

So we have presented the problem: you think you are your primary instrument, and your primary instrument needs a bit of work if you are going to succeed in life, particularly if you want to free yourself from attachment.

Karma yoga, or *dharma yoga,* is explained extensively in Chapters XIII and XIV of my book *The Essence of Enlightenment,* so I will only present a synopsis here. It is the basic preparation for the Yoga of the Three Energies.

I have emotional problems because life is not giving me what I want, meaning my primary instrument is dominated by *rajas* and *tamas.* If it was predominately *sattvic*, it would serve me well and I would accomplish my goals without a lot of fuss. *Karma yoga* transforms a dull (*tamasic*) and excessively active (*rajasic*) mind into a clear, peaceful, efficient (*sattvic*) mind. The basic logic is good for *samsaris* who want to accomplish worldly goals, but the full version is mandatory for people who want freedom from *samsara*. Without it self-knowledge will not stick. It works on the doer, the part of the subtle body that owns action and that acts only to enjoy the ostensible results. When you act for results, you incur stress before, during and after the action. *Karma yoga* removes stress by undoing the fears and desires that produce it. It is burnout insurance.

A Glaring Downside

Wanting things is fine, but it suffers one glaring downside: the results of your actions are not up to you. It is amazing how thoroughly this simple fact irritates the doer. But think about it: if the results of your actions were up to you, you would have everything you want. So what are the results up to? The law of *karma* in the form of the *dharma* field, my immediate environment, basically the people with whom I have *karma*. My primary instrument generates actions which affect the field, a conscious matrix of laws. The actions I do return to me in various, not always obvious, ways. My life is nothing but the results of actions I have done before, delivered to me by the field. The field is impersonal and delivers the results of the actions of individuals based on the needs of the field itself. It doesn't care what I want, unless what I want serves the field in some way.

In terms of my happiness, the field is all-powerful. My dependence on it causes suffering. I cannot just walk away from it, because there isn't anywhere else to go.

My desires command me to act. Even if I run off to a cave in India, my desires torture me there. Better to stay here and work them out in such a way that they don't come back. They come back because the needy attitude that motivates them doesn't disappear when I get what I want. As soon as I get one thing, I want something else. *Karma yoga* is an attitude with reference to action that removes unnecessary desire.

An Attitude of Gratitude

Because I value life more than anything and because it is a gift from the field of existence, I reciprocate by taking the three *dharmas* into account and offering my actions as a gift to the field. *Karma yoga* is a giving, not a getting, attitude.

It is the appropriate response to life's demands. It breaks the hold of *rajasic* and *tamasic* desires, and converts an extroverted, emotional mind into a peaceful, introspective, *sattvic* mind.

What you do with the gift of life is your offering to the field. The field is obviously intelligently designed, so there has to be an intelligent architect. And the field controls us completely, right down to causing us to breathe, to eat and digest our food, so it is called God. What we do with the gift of life is our offering to God.

If you appreciate this fact, which should be second nature, you will not offer a greedy, angry, vain, licentious life to Life. You will offer a pure life as a wonderful gift with a cheerful, smiling face. You may wonder why, considering the downsides of life, that you should present a cheerful, smiling face. However, if you are fair-minded, you can find an upside for every downside because life is a perfectly equilibrated duality. The half-empty glass is half-full. A positive attitude is no less realistic than a negative attitude.

The best life is not a material life, because it does not tap our real potential, and it is a life of problems that tends to compromise our authenticity. The best life is a sincere life, one that manifests our innate spiritual potential and adds real value to the world. To do what you love is the best worship you can offer, assuming it doesn't involve injury.

How does *karma yoga* work? Before I act, I offer the actions to the field, and when results come, which they do every minute, I take them as a gift, even if they aren't what I want, in which case I see them as instructive, corrective offerings from the field that help me to avoid actions that will produce unwanted results in the future. In this way I set up healthy communications with my environment.

Of course it is not easy, because the ego, the most *tamasic* function in the subtle body, abhors change and does not like to relinquish the idea of control, even though it is not in control of the results in the first place. Rather than follow the foolish advice of *gurus* who tout ego death, you need to make friends with your ego and educate it, not eradicate it, not that ego death is even possible. Enlightened or not, you cannot function in the world without an ego. If you patiently educate your ego in the *karma yoga* spirit, it will like you because you have given it good, noble work, and you will like it because it will stop being a problem.

The Five Offerings

Karma yoga is not only right attitude, it is right action. Actions can be classified in terms of how well they serve to prepare the mind for inquiry.

They are (1) *sattvic*, those that give maximum spiritual benefit, (2) *rajasic*, those that are neither beneficial nor detrimental, and (3) *tamasic*, those that are harmful and lead one away from the goal.

Tamasic Karmas

These actions build unhelpful *vasanas* that take the doer away from liberation. Violence in thought, word and deed, lying, cheating, stealing, gambling, drinking alcohol, taking drugs, excessive sex solely for pleasure, etc. are examples of the third class of *karmas*. They are considered sins because they produce a dull and agitated mind. They are not recommended for anyone and are definitely prohibited for *karma yogis*.

Rajasic Karmas

The second class is desire-prompted activities that basically contribute to our material well-being. These activities do not directly contribute to preparing the mind, but they are scripturally sanctioned because they indirectly make it possible to pursue liberation. They are not considered sins as long as they do not compel the individual to violate *dharma* or ignore the legitimate needs of others, in which case they increase selfishness, a detrimental characteristic. In fact the Vedic scriptures prescribe a number of rituals for getting money, property, certain types of children, etc. They are not encouraged or discouraged.

Sattvic Karmas

The first class of actions, *sattvic karmas*, are necessary if *karma yoga* is going to bear fruit. They are giving *karmas*, not grabbing *karmas*. The more you give, the more you grow. *Karma yoga* involves actions that add value to every situation, offerings that contribute to the well-being of the *dharma* field.

The intention of a *karma yogi* is to enshrine *sattvic karmas* at the forefront of her life, to see that *rajasic karmas* are relegated to subordinate status and to eliminate *tamasic karmas*. Of course it is impossible to eliminate *tamasic* actions altogether. Certain situations demand them. *Sattvic karmas* bring about maturity and spiritual growth. These actions are not based on desires for tangible results like money, fame, status, pleasure, children and so forth. They should be considered compulsory actions – assuming the desire for liberation.

What are these *karmas*? They are called the Five Essential Contributions. There is no tangible benefit from them. One of these practices does not replace the other. Just as eating only dessert at the expense of nutritious foods is not enough, all five are necessary. Each one affects a different part of the psyche, and the psyche as a whole needs to be healed. These practices are the essence of *karma yoga* because they directly contribute to spiritual growth.

1. **Worship of God in any form.** *Isvara/Maya*, the Creator of the *dharma* field, is God. *Karma yoga* is worship of God. Most modern spiritual people have abandoned religion because so much suffering has been foisted on the human race in its name. But the religious impulse, the Self loving itself, is as hardwired as the desire for identity. So it is incumbent on a *karma yogi* to choose a symbol of the Self that is attractive and uplifting, and worship it regularly. It can be anything because every object is just God in a particular form. It may be a ritual in front of an idol or a photo. It can be telling the beads, visiting a temple, doing service or giving money to a church or mosque.

2. **Unconditional reverence for parents,** especially difficult ones. For instance, if you don't feel love when you think of your parents, you should inquire into why you have a problem with them. You should "heal" the relationship in your mind by understanding.

If your parent could have been different, he or she would have been different in that he or she did their best according to their conditioning. Find a place in your heart to accommodate them and give them credit for the good qualities they instilled in you. They are no longer in your life, physically perhaps, but they are still in your mind. They are part of it and it is made out of you. Until you have a loving feeling about that part of your mind, you will not be free to inquire properly. In any case, the essence of enlightenment is love, so you might as well start somewhere. Once you have dissolved the negativity, bring an image of them into your mind and fill the image with love. Keep the love flowing to the image as long as possible.

3. **Worship of scriptures.** The purpose of *karma yoga* is to cultivate devotion, develop your understanding and gain a contemplative disposition so that you can assimilate the meaning of the teachings. You should not think that you will start inquiry one fine day when you are contemplative. You should set aside half an hour, an hour or more daily for study of Vedanta.

Pick a text, read a verse or a few pages each morning and contemplate throughout the day. You don't become contemplative all at once. You have contemplative moments throughout the day and insights all along. Cultivate those moments, and the extroverted mind will gradually turn inward.

4. **Service to humanity.** Worshipful service simply means responding appropriately to legitimate, small, everyday requests for help. When someone wants something from you, see if you can't accommodate them, assuming it is a reasonable desire. If you are helping others, at least you are not wasting your

time indulging your own *tamasic* and *rajasic* habits. Service isn't only doing what others want, although it might include that. It is showing an accommodating openness to others, not shutting them out.

Because ego, born of a sense of inadequacy and inferiority, looks for opportunities to feel special, virtuous and recognized, humble service keeps these tendencies in check. It is based on a recognition of the essential oneness of all. It is also wise because everything we need comes through others. Service-oriented individuals are generally well looked after.

5. **Worship of all sentient beings.** There is no distance between us and nature. We are born in it, live in it and die in it. Worshiping nature is continual mindfulness of our environments, beautifying them and contributing to them always, including the body, our most intimate contact with nature. How we relate to everything in our delicately balanced ecosystem has a powerful effect on our state of mind. Recycle. Reduce your carbon footprint. Go green. Vegetarianism is a good way to worship life.

Chapter VII

Devotion

What's Love Got to Do with It?

Before we get too deeply into the topic of the *gunas*, we need to introduce the topic of love because we don't just need to engage our fears, our *tamasic* energy, we need to engage our desires, our *rajasic* energy.

Fear of *samsara* – the "jaws of the crocodile," as it is humorously called in Vedic literature – is a good motivator, but fear's upside, desire, is even better. Although love is not desire, desire is love. Fear of bondage is love of freedom, and freedom from bondage is unconditional self-love.

And since the world is the Self, transcendence of the *gunas* is unconditional love of the world, meaning my body, mind and intellect, which are part and parcel of the world.

But when I begin my spiritual life, I'm conflicted about my relationship with the world. On one hand, I love specific parts of it, insofar as everything I love belongs to the world: "my" body, spouse, kids, job, house, pets, etc. But loving it this way creates unwanted attachment, which is painful.

It is wise to love the world, since everything we love comes from it. But wise people don't love the world in the same way worldly people love it. They love it as an impersonal field of energies on which we depend for our very existence.

They love God, the cause of the world, which is called *bhakti*, devotion. So *karma yoga*, offering my actions to the world in a spirit of love, is devotional *yoga. Yoga* means "union" or "connection." It connects my heart to God because the world is non-separate from its Creator. Yes, desire is love, but it is a selfish form of love that binds me to the material and psychological aspects of God and needs to be transformed into devotion, a selfless, liberating love. Loving God with attachment is not a problem like the love of specific objects created by God, because God is free, always present and non-separate from me, the Self, not to mention that God's nature is love, so there is no pain involved. We should not fail to mention once more that loving the cause includes all its effects, so the objects that God presents to me get loved by default without causing attachment.

Karma yoga is the first stage of the transformation of love. To practice it I need to have enough *sattva* to appreciate that the fact that a quiet mind is

69

necessary for self-knowledge and that self-knowledge converts conditional love into liberating, unconditional, *guna*-free devotion.

At the same time, my love is still contaminated by *rajas* and *tamas*, love of

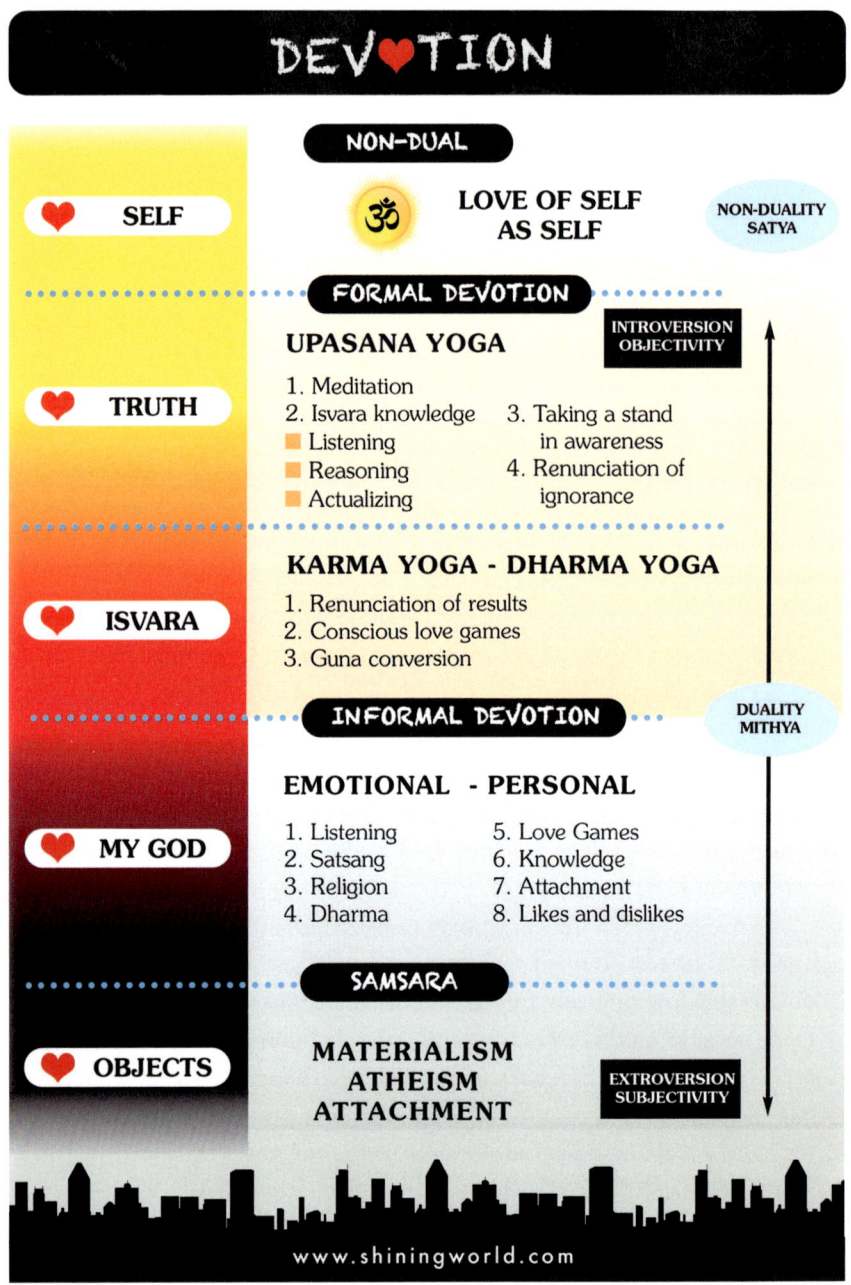

DEV♥TION

NON-DUAL

♥ **SELF**

🕉 **LOVE OF SELF AS SELF**

NON-DUALITY SATYA

FORMAL DEVOTION

INTROVERSION OBJECTIVITY

UPASANA YOGA

♥ **TRUTH**

1. Meditation
2. Isvara knowledge
   - Listening
   - Reasoning
   - Actualizing
3. Taking a stand in awareness
4. Renunciation of ignorance

KARMA YOGA - DHARMA YOGA

♥ **ISVARA**

1. Renunciation of results
2. Conscious love games
3. Guna conversion

INFORMAL DEVOTION

DUALITY MITHYA

EMOTIONAL - PERSONAL

♥ **MY GOD**

1. Listening
2. Satsang
3. Religion
4. Dharma
5. Love Games
6. Knowledge
7. Attachment
8. Likes and dislikes

SAMSARA

♥ **OBJECTS**

MATERIALISM ATHEISM ATTACHMENT

EXTROVERSION SUBJECTIVITY

www.shiningworld.com

God's stuff. Yes, God's stuff is God, but God is not God's stuff, so eventually I need to love God apart from God's stuff. In the meantime, however, *karma yoga* permits me to love according to my predominant *guna*, insofar as it is impossible to convert *tamas* and *rajas* into *sattva*, and *sattva* into *guna*-free devotion, overnight. So *karma yoga* has two stages: love with desire and love without desire. Both fall under the topic of *guna bhakti*.

Love with Desire ~ *Rajas* and *Tamas*

When devotion is selfish, it is difficult to take one's angers and disappointments as a gift from God as *karma yoga* recommends. Because we are emotionally immature, at this stage we include God in our prayers for no other reason than we appreciate the fact that God is in charge of the distribution of stuff. This rudimentary devotion is not particularly noble, but it's okay because at least it includes God in the conversation and builds self-esteem. You like yourself when you acknowledge your dependence on God because it is the truth. Without God, your self-esteem is always under attack because you only love yourself when you are getting what you want, a foolish basis for self-worth since life doesn't care if you get what you want. Without compunction, it will just as well deny your desires as affirm them. Dependence on anything except God is not wonderful, but thinking you are alone is sheer ignorance. If you worship God by acting in harmony with its laws, you quickly discover a very helpful friend. So acknowledging your dependence on God is a necessary baby step toward freedom.

Love of Gods' stuff does not remove anxiety (*rajas*) and depression (*tamas*), but taking them as God's will slowly neutralize them.

Praying for the well-being of others is a way out of this stage because it requires an appreciation of the fact that we are all in the same leaky boat, navigating our way across the turbulent ocean of *samsara*. By definition this type of devotion is *tamasic*. The devotee may mechanically repeat a favorite name of God without understanding who he or she is talking to. Because they can't think clearly, *tamasic* devotees are prone to fantasy. They may believe that one circumambulation of a holy mountain on a full moon night or one million repetitions of a special *mantra* is sufficient for liberation. This kind of devotion is encouraged in the secondary Vedic literature, the *Puranas*, but only as a starting point.

Love without Desire ~ Sublimating *Rajas* and *Tamas* into *Sattva*

In this stage, desire for worldly things is not allowed, only prayer for the courage and strength to take both positive and negative results as a gift from *Isvara*, the law of *karma*. The devotee is not aiming for a particular experience. There is desire, but the desire is for peace of mind. This stage purifies likes and dislikes because when a conflict arises one goes with what *Isvara*, one's situation, demands, not what one wants. The devotee stops treating God as a problem-solver and stops blaming God for his bad *karma*.

Obviously, from the non-dual perspective any service given is the Self giving service to itself, but in the second stage the extroverted devotee is trying to purify selfishness, so he asks God to help the world, not himself. This stage breeds saints. It is not an easy stage, because the devotee is praying for the strength to resist worldly desires. In the first stage you may have realized that desiring objects isn't healthy, but you are still attached to them. At the same time, you know that to love God unconditionally your heart must be pure.

Devotees in the second stage staff monasteries, churches and temples, and do a rudimentary form of *karma yoga* without understanding the nuances of its logic. Since the *karma* they do accrues to the accounts of others, they don't accumulate *rajasic* and *tamasic* tendencies, and they accrue a *sattvic* tendency for service, often tainted with vanity, which can bind like any other. Most large spiritual and religious organizations are built on the backs of this kind of devotee. They believe that when all their *karmas* are burned up by good deeds enlightenment will ensue. On the kitchen wall of a very wealthy *ashram* I observed this sign: "One hour of dishwashing burns one lifetime of *karma!*" Obviously, the *guru* did not understand that action won't burn ignorance or that *moksa* means burning the doer in the fire of self-knowledge.

Love of Inner Work ~ More *Sattva*, Less *Rajas* and *Tamas*

The *karma yoga* stages convert an extroverted mind into an introverted mind. In the meditation phase there is a gradual reduction of worldly activities and an increase of mental activity. Because one's thoughts are now going to a symbol of the Self – symbols invoke their referents and the Self is unconditional love (*parama prema*) – the devotee experiences love without reference to objects and events.

In this stage the devotee bonds with *Isvara* and nourishes his relationship with *Isvara*. He no longer depends on relationships for love – family and friends – but draws on *Isvara* for emotional support. This stage removes fear. The goal of spiritual life is to see God, the Self, in everything, but non-dual vision – which amounts to non-dual love – requires a very subtle mind. At this stage the devotee's mind is not expansive enough to gain that vision, so he or she worships a specific symbol of God that stands for the total, an *ishta devata*.

Worship of Everything ~ Predominant Sattva

This, the penultimate stage, further expands and purifies the mind. It removes likes and dislikes: jealousy, hatred, possessiveness, etc. There is still duality – relationship – in this stage, but the "person" to whom one relates is the conscious being that is everything.

Seeing the divinity in particular objects that excite one's love for God is well and good, but seeing the divine in all objects is the goal. In this stage the devotee must drill down into every object appearing in his consciousness until he can see consciousness – his own innermost Self – shining there. Chapter IX of the *Gita* presents the Self in its creative aspect as a cosmic universal person, someone that is both wonderful and terrifying, the idea being that the devotee should love the ugly, angry, fearful parts of his or her Self and accept the evil in the world as an inevitable consequence of self-ignorance. The holy parts of one's Self are easy to love, the dark parts less so. As long as differences exist in the devotee's mind, love is conditional.

Emotional Impact of the "Vision" of the Total

This vision instills a sense of reverence and love for everything because everything is nothing but the Self of the devotee. It causes wonderment: How can something and its opposite be me? At the same time, it generates fear because it involves the acceptance of the inevitable losses that are part and parcel of the fabric of life. It is complete when the devotee happily accepts the demise of all objects, particularly the body and loved ones. At this stage the devotee sees every action as worship of the Lord and does not care about the results of actions, because his sole purpose it to arrive at stage five.

The Fruit of Devotion ~ Non-Duality, Pure Sattva

Chapter X discusses this topic in detail.

Chapter VIII
Self-Inquiry

WE DON'T COUNT devotion as a special path, because everything everyone does is motivated by love. Worldly people love the world and their desires for objects. Religious people love their personal deities, *karma yogis* love God as the giver of the results of their actions, and self-inquirers love self-inquiry because it leads to liberation, which leads to unconditional self-love, which they love above everything.

Karma yoga, however, is a particular discipline, a formal path which may seem quite daunting. Perhaps there is a fast track? Why not just skip *karma yoga* and go directly to self-inquiry? Because you can't gain self-knowledge if you have a lot of worldly *karma*. If you weren't attached to your life as your desires and fears have structured it, you would just immediately walk away into a simple, pure, *sattvic* life of inquiry with no regrets, but worldly *karma* makes the mind emotional and intellectually dull. Self-inquiry is a very subtle discipline requiring great patience, dispassion and commitment because its concepts are counter-intuitive.

Yes, you may pick up a few workable ideas here and there, but as long as your desires and fears keep pushing and pulling you around, you will take a step backward – sometimes two – for every step forward. Like *karma yoga,* self-inquiry is a discipline. It is keeping one eye on the Self and one eye on your mind as you manage your life. Self-inquiry is only suitable for individuals with little worldly *karma*.

Karma yoga is an entry-level course on *Isvara. Jnana yoga* – self-inquiry – is advanced study. It is PhD-level knowledge of *Isvara*. As your knowledge of *Isvara* grows, your love of *Isvara* grows. When you discover that you are non-separate from *Isvara*, you discover that you are the bliss that you formerly sought in objects, which means that you are free of *samsara*, dependence on objects, for your happiness.

Importance of a Values Inventory

The first stage of *jnana yoga* is an analysis of values. If your values conform to your goals, little work is required because your primary instrument will automatically line up with your highest values. Inquiry doesn't work if non-conforming priorities are in play. If they are, aligning your values with your goals is hard work. For instance, if you are lazy, have a strong *rajasic* value for wealth and you are equally burdened with a *sattvic* attachment to honesty, it may be wise to ditch the honesty value and cultivate a *tamasic* value for deceit insofar as honesty compels you to play by the rules, whereas if you appreciate the value of a lie or a partial lie, many more avenues for quick riches open up. This is not to say that the downside of deceit, constant fear of exposure and the consequences, will not grind the edge off your happiness unless you are a truly sociopathic personality. However, if you have a strong *sattvic* value for self-knowledge because you want freedom and you have a value for lying, you need to jettison the *tamasic* value because self-inquiry requires ruthless integrity.

If you pursue self-knowledge because *rajasic* and *tamasic* values cause suffering and you realize that you are the Self, the fruit of self-realization – perfect satisfaction – will elude you until you align your values with *dharma*.

Irrespective of this fact, many so-called enlightened *gurus* falsely claim that because they are beyond the *gunas* they can violate *dharma* with impunity, but suffering is inevitable for lawbreakers because *Isvara* hardwires *dharma* into the subtle body of every *jiva,* enlightened or not. The spiritual world is rife with once glorious but deceitful and abusive personalities whom *Isvara,* in the form of the *dharma* field, reduced to pathetic, broken shadows of their former selves. Complicity in the form of *tamasic* gullibility on the part of devotees worldwide accounts for the perennial presence of *adharmic* religious and spiritual cults.

This is not to say that a committed person cannot practice self-inquiry and values-adjustment simultaneously. However, if self-inquiry stops bearing fruit, non-conforming values must be eliminated before growth resumes.

Develop Conforming Values: Renounce Non-Conforming Values

So what values align with self-inquiry and what values impede it? We will take up the positive values first because it is impossible to justify attachment to negative values when you experience the bliss of positive values. Remember, *Isvara* is pure *sattva* before *rajas* and *tamas* predominate. *Rajas* and *tamas* contaminate *jiva,* not *Isvara.* Every time you invoke a positive value, you align yourself with *Isvara,* the bliss sheath, and you feel good. This feeling is the basis of lasting self-esteem.

Values inventory is not for self-judgment, nor for judgment of others, but for understanding each value so well that you and your understanding are non-different. Then, if you are fully committed to freedom, any tendency that conflicts with the values structure required for inquirers needs to be extirpated. Values kept as ideals create conflict because they produce a sense of inauthenticity.

Trying to live up to an ideal prevents you from dealing with your *rajas* and *tamas* in the here and now because no matter how *sattvic* you become, you will never be satisfied, since all *jivas* are flawed. Only the Self is perfect. Failure to appreciate this fact may cause considerable suffering, not only with reference to your relationship to yourself but with your relationship to others, particularly spiritual authorities. All gods have feet of clay.

As long as the choices we make do not conflict with our highest values, convenient, expedient choices are encouraged, not just sanctioned. The hair shirt is an unpleasant, unnecessarily *tamasic* idea. Convenience, however, is not the main criterion for choice. If it goes against certain values, we do only what is to be done, not what is convenient. Just as *karma yoga* is a discipline that breaks the tendency to act without thinking, all disciplines demand constant remembrance of our highest value, in our case the bliss of liberation.

Cultivate These Values

In terms of action, the definition of *sattva* is: doing only those things that need to be done according to the situation, not according to your likes and dislikes. When you know who you are, all activities are reduced to duties. There is no excitement or fear concerning what has to be done, because you are full and complete. You know that you cannot be enhanced or diminished by the performance of any action.

Yes, inquiry demands sacrifice when a like or dislike is not in keeping with *dharma*, but every time you let go you experience the bliss of *sattva* and you understand that what you gave up is less valuable since it was for the sake of bliss that your like or dislike was operating in the first place! Renunciation of likes and dislikes creates self-confidence, and self-confidence makes you more objective; over time dispassion becomes a natural part of your personality.

Spiritual growth requires a suitable infrastructure, but since such an infrastructure is not available in materialistic societies, you have to create a simple, *sattvic* lifestyle yourself.

A clear understanding of *Isvara*, the *dharma* field, brings the *jiva* into a relationship with *Isvara* that makes the mind *sattvic*. Without this connection the *jiva* cannot express *Isvara's* positive qualities. A *dharmic* life is a life in harmony with the whole. The following *sattva*-generating values purify *rajas* and *tamas*. To investigate them is to cultivate them. The practice of these virtues enables one to become free from the effects of ignorance. The result is happiness.

1. RESOLUTION OF INNER CONFLICT

Most of us are well aware of our messy, conflicted minds and would like to resolve our issues but, owing to the pursuit of worldly ends – security, pleasure, recognition, power, etc. – we don't value peace of mind enough to pursue it. If there is no value apart from lip service for integrating the three limbs of the subtle body – the mind, intellect and ego – into a harmonious whole, inquiry is impossible.

2. Self-Confidence

The pursuit of material goals leads to binding *vasanas,* putting the *jiva* at the mercy of its fears and desires, producing inner conflict and sapping its sense of self-worth. Low self-esteem is so widespread these days that it has become a talking point designed to elicit sympathy. It's one thing to understand your problems, and quite another to do something about them.

You may temporarily feel good when you get what you want, but good feelings do not amount to self-esteem.

Self-esteem is a sustained sense of self-worth developed by doing what is right for your growth, which isn't going to happen unless you have a strong value for self-mastery. Backed by self-knowledge, every time you stand up to and dismiss a useless fear or desire your sense of self-love increases.

3. Steadiness

Steadiness in inquiry is one of the most important *sattvic* values because it resolves emotional problems directly by attacking the thoughts that produce them, turning negative emotions into positive emotions. Yes, *karma yoga* produces *sattva* and builds self-esteem, but it works its magic more slowly. This value implies a value for devotion to God and to the study of Vedanta scriptures.

4. Non-Injury

There is a universal value for non-injury because nobody wants to be hurt. Non-injury is a nuanced value difficult to apply, owing to the nature of the world in which we live. Three categories of injury prevail: actions, words and thoughts. The most obvious expression of an injurious action is physical violence.

A common expression of non-injury favored by spiritual types is vegetarianism. The argument is: although life eats life, human beings are not in the same choiceless category as animals, whose food is dictated by instinct. We are self-conscious and endowed with free will, and since there are many means of survival, we are free to choose a non-ambulatory food source. Although plants are living beings, they are not conscious as animals are, so eating grains, fruits and vegetables is morally superior to killing conscious beings. Swami Dayananda, a great champion of vegetarianism, says, "To bring meat-eating in line with *dharma* I would have to kill my prey bare-handed, thus exposing myself to the possibility of becoming some animal's dinner.

"If I am not willing to do this, I am little more than an unethical, cowardly hypocrite owing to an incompletely assimilated value for non-injury revealed by my failure to risk the possibility of suffering the same result the animal risks."

For many, vegetarianism is sufficient as far as the value for non-injury is concerned, but the definition of non-injury includes two other types of *karma*: thoughts and words. Words should be truthful and pleasing. White lies are okay in certain situations because compassion trumps honesty. Our sensitivity to violence needs to include a careful consideration of the effects of our words on others and the effects of harmful thoughts on our own minds. You may think that your bad feelings are justified by the *adharmic* behavior of others, but they do not punish the offender or make the situation right; they serve only to hurt your own mind.

It is a shame that since the sixties, when hedonistic individualism became acceptable, society became increasingly disturbed and the traditions of civility, manners particularly, gradually declined. The solution to negative thoughts and actions is to develop an appreciation of the feelings of others because, considering the non-dual nature of reality, there are no others. "Others" is only an idea in an ignorant mind. To develop such an appreciation, I need to look beyond my own needs and develop an appreciation for the feelings of others. Such an attitude is conducive to self-inquiry insofar as neither inner nor outer conflict is conducive to self-inquiry.

5. STRAIGHTFORWARDNESS, TRUTHFULNESS

Alignment of thought, word and deed is straightforwardness. Saying one thing and doing something else is not conducive to peace of mind and inquiry. Straightforwardness includes not only truthful speech, but thought and actions. Non-alignment fragments the person, subjecting him to a disturbed mind.

6. DISPASSION TOWARD SENSE OBJECTS

An extremely important value that amounts to existential maturity, dispassion, is defined as a clear appreciation of two hard-to-assimilate facts: (1) the joy I seek is not to be found in objects and (2) life is a zero-sum game. It strips away false emotion created by my tendencies and presents the world as an objective fact to my mind. It is also indifference to the results of my actions.

7. Fearlessness

There is no evidence whatsoever that you die, unless you think you are the body. Death is only the thought "I will die one day," which produces fear. *Tamas* hides the thought, and *rajas* sends the attention to the emotion. Because I can't see the thought and own it, I blame circumstances for the bad feeling.

When you detect the thought "I will die one day," inquire into it. What is it that dies? The body? Yes, it is definitely going to die; nothing can stop it. The body is born of the *tamasic* aspect of the five elements. *Tamas* is entropy, a natural degenerative factor. The body is also an assemblage, which is subject to disintegration. In any case, I am not the body, because the body is an object known to me. This simple logic is discrimination, which is merely a value for common sense.

Inquiry brings about a cognitive change so that the thought of death either does not come or, if it does, the neutralizing logic arises along with it. We have to create "antibodies" in our minds to deal with these fears as they arise. So when the "I will die" thought arises, look on the bright side: "That I am alive today is a matter for celebration."

What will happen tomorrow is another fear-thought. But if we look back, we have been surviving all these years, in spite of this fear. To neutralize it, understand that you need only to deal with one day at a time. Knowing just how little is required to survive should take care of fear of the future.

Fear does not change the fact that change is a fact. Welcome it, as every change is an opportunity; fear contracts the subtle body and prevents growth.

8. Honesty ~ Straightforwardness

I don't lie to you because I don't want to be lied to. I lie because I think I have something to gain by lying or something to lose by telling the truth. If you think you have something to gain or lose in this life, you don't know who you are. When your mind is clear, you can see the downside of lying, whereas a cloudy, disturbed mind is prone to seeing value where none exists. *Rajas* and *tamas* often pressure the mind to make expedient, morally irresponsible decisions.

Again, straightforwardness is alignment of thought, word and deed. Saying one thing and doing another or doing something and saying something else is not conducive to peace of mind and inquiry. Straightforwardness includes not only truthful speech, but thought and actions too. Non-alignment subjects the mind to restlessness. Because you are conscious of *dharma* when your mind is *sattvic*, your words won't conceal your intentions and actions.

9. UNSWERVING NON-DUAL DEVOTION TO GOD

We refer to awareness as *Isvara,* not pure consciousness, in the discussion of values because values are only an issue for someone who does not know who they are, so the devotion mentioned here is not hard and fast self-knowledge. It is an understanding that a *jiva* seeking freedom would do well to assume, as it produces the steadiness of mind mentioned in the last value.

Karma yoga practice is a natural by-product of non-dual devotion, an attitude of grateful acceptance brought about by seeing *Isvara* as the giver of the results of actions. Like inquiry, it frees the mind of projections and brings it in line with objective reality, making the assimilation of the teachings possible.

10. NON-STEALING

Non-stealing literally means non-stealing, as well as any benefit derived through unfair transactions, false advertising, concealing information, etc.

11. CLEANLINESS, PURITY

Swami Dayananda says: "Even as I go about my business every day, a little dust settles on my skin, some dirt stains my clothes, my desk becomes littered, my mind gathers dust in its transactions with people. Smudges of envy settle, a spot of exasperation lands, streaks of possessiveness appear and overall a fine dust of self-criticism, guilt and self-condemnation spreads. Each day, until my false identification with the mind dissolves and self-knowledge arises, the mind must be cleaned."

The detergent for the mind is applying the opposite thought. A resentment settles in your mind, especially if you were legitimately wronged, but don't allow it to remain, as it will grow into hate. To wash the mind, deliberately look for reasons to like the person that harmed you. He is liked by others, loved by his wife, takes care of his children properly, gives to charity and goes to church on Sunday.

Everyone is capable of love; even criminals love their children and sympathize with their friends. Blame the person's *rajasic* and *tamasic* qualities on wrong thinking caused by a bad environment. Think: "There but for the grace of God go I," and be happy.

Selfishness is a dirty thought. When you see that you are indifferent to the needs of others, create a serving *vasana* by deliberately doing an unselfish action. Likewise, self-condemnation is a dirty thought. When things go wrong or you contravene a norm and you feel guilty and ashamed, show compassion for yourself and assert you true nature: "I am whole and complete, non-dual love."

Bring to mind the understanding that the body and mind are innocent, that they are programmed by *vasanas* born of unconscious actions and attitudes.

Understand this logic based on the teaching: saintly qualities belong to *sattva*. No one is without *sattva*, so I have *sattva*. *Sattva* is the pure reflection of the Self, the eternal *Jiva*. I am that *Jiva*. The *Jiva* is non-separate from *Isvara*, who is pure love. Therefore I am whole and complete love. *Rajasic* and *tamasic* qualities which cause selfishness are incidental; they come and go. They are not me. I am just fine.

12. PURITY

Purity is allowing anyone access to your thoughts because you have nothing to hide. You are not embarrassed by the uncharitable content of your mind. People who try to protect their thoughts are insecure and harbor negative thoughts about others.

13. CHASTITY

Chastity is maintaining a respectful attitude towards members of the opposite sex, not abstinence from sex.

14. ORDER, SIMPLICITY

An orderly mind is a fundamental prerequisite for self-knowledge. A disordered mind is a consequence of uninformed seeking. Like chickens with their heads cut off, seekers hop from teacher to teacher and from one path to another, indiscriminately picking up confusing bits of wisdom and ignorance until their minds are so completely cluttered with senseless ideas they are unsure if they are coming or going.

Inquiry is not seeking. Seeking stops and inquiry begins when Vedanta finds you. It is a common-sense, complete, scientific understanding of the fundamental order of existence, a logical set of proven principles that invariably simplifies the mind and prepares it to assimilate the knowledge that sets you free. If the mind is orderly, orderly eating, sleeping, working and recreational habits necessary for a simple life follow.

15. Accommodation, Commodiousness

To cheerfully and calmly accept any type of person or a given situation, not resigned indifference, is accommodation. It is based on a clear understanding that things cannot be different from the way they are, owing to the law of *karma*. Behavior is a consequence of conditioning and not subject to willpower. We are incarnated to work out *karma*, not to manipulate *karma* to conform to likes and dislikes. Situations are the result of all the factors in the *dharma* field and are beyond the control of individuals; it is foolish to like or dislike them. Successful relationships depend on accommodation. Similarly, I cannot be different from what I am, and my situation is the result of my *karma*, so I should cheerfully accommodate my apparent self, not place undue demands on it.

To develop this important quality, I should learn to appreciate variety, cultivate an attitude of diversity and constantly monitor my mind for a sense of dissatisfaction. When I become aware that I am dissatisfied, I should reduce my expectations. It is helpful to see myself and everyone else as helpless fools or inert objects. I have good relationships with inert objects because I expect nothing of them. I suffer fools gladly because I know they cannot be otherwise.

The key to accommodation is to respond to and identify with the person, not their actions. Understand that the person is the Self temporarily bewitched by *Maya*. Try to remember that *Isvara* is behind an angry outburst, a fit of jealousy or a domineering action, and appreciate the fact that if others have no control, you have even less. With this kind of understanding it is easy to become accommodative.

16. Charity (Gifting, Not Grifting)

Responsible giving implies an inquiry into the motivations for giving. If you don't feel virtuous, you may be inclined to compensate by giving, and if the virtue gap is huge, you may give more than is appropriate, compromising your own financial situation, making you dependent on others. Giving to impress or control others is not charity. Motiveless giving, however, destroys greed, one of the many gates to suffering. Motiveless giving comes from *Isvara*. It springs from an uncalculated, natural empathy and is not tinged with regret.

Charity given at the right time and place with respect, considering the needs of the recipient, is *sattvic*. Joyless, ostentatious charity given to make oneself feel generous is *rajasic*. Inappropriate and inconsiderate gifts given at the wrong place and time is *tamasic*.

The best gift is the gift of love. At the same time, love makes any material gift, no matter how small, meaningful. When you sincerely pay attention to others without interpreting their words before they have finished speaking, you grow quickly. If you can't give without making the recipient feel beholden, give anonymously. Put things on the street where anyone can grab them and feel blessed by fate. If your ego is uncharitable, remember that life is a zero-sum game; the heart that gives gathers. Your "loss" is actually a gain.

17. Gratitude

If you feel hard done by life and your mind is accustomed to complaining about your sorry lot, you need get down to the basics and appreciate the very fact that you want to live another day indicates a great love of life. It is a gift that should be appreciated every waking minute.

18. Satisfaction

Satisfaction is cultivating an abundant, charitable, composed state of mind. It is contentment with what we have and letting go of beggarly, possessive attitudes. It is sharing what one has – time, money and attention. It neutralizes *rajas'* signature energy, dissatisfaction.

19. Ability to Resolve Anger

Anger is anguish arising out of unfulfilled expectations. Maintaining it is masochistic because you have the option of changing the thought that is producing it. If you are angry with your spouse, for instance, remind yourself of the reason you fell in love in the first place; that reason is always valid. Rediscover it.

Number-two son got hand-me-downs when he was young and resents his parents, which makes contact with them unpleasant. His parents didn't buy new items, because they were saving money for his college education. He graduated and got a good job. Therefore their frugality was a blessing. Women can only give birth serially, except in the case of twins, etc., so it is not his mother's fault that he was number two. His mother went through back-to-back pregnancies so he would have a big brother when he was growing up. He was lucky because his big brother stood up for him when he was in trouble.

Swami Dayananda says: "Cognitively we can change because anger, like every other emotion, is preceded by a conclusive thought, like, 'This is never going to happen to me,' or, 'I can never make him understand.' Thoughts like these are the missing link between old anger and the current situation. This thought is mechanical and usually goes undetected. It happens without your permission. Any situation which reminds you of the cause of your original anger can trigger the thought, and once the thought has come the anger is there. There is no feeling without these conclusive thoughts. They hold the anger, and therefore by proper inquiry we can neutralize it."

20. RENUNCIATION, AUSTERITY, RESTRAINT, SELF-CONTROL

It would be difficult to find a more useful value than renunciation. World War II post-war prosperity has created societies chock to the brim with needy, wanting creatures: "I want what I want the way I want it and I want it NOW!" This attitude, inspired by the wholesale spiritual emptiness of huge populations, has produced an intensity and volume of disturbing thoughts that is unprecedented in human history. The solution: cultivate a value for renunciation. The holy *mantra* of the renunciant is "less is more." The fewer gross and subtle objects I crave and possess, the more peace I enjoy.

Austerity is building and conserving energy by restraining non-essential desires and indulging in energy-creating activities, self-inquiry, for instance. Individuals with predominant *rajas* often consign themselves to a life of debt or a hand-to-mouth existence, owing to a lack of this value. Money is energy. Saving money is prudent and generates *sattva*, peace. If you don't have a financial cushion appropriate to your station in life, your peace of mind will be continually compromised. However, if you are blessed with spirit of renunciation, the loss of objects does not disturb you.

The *rajas/tamas* syndrome inclines an individual to sentimentality, which inevitably involves petty impulse buying that seems innocent enough in the short run but which deplete resources in the long run. If you have to gift every relative on every occasion, pamper yourself with massages, clothing and dinners out because you're "worth it" or to keep up with the Joneses, know that your value for austerity is virtually non-existent. If every square inch of your home, including closets, drawers and the garage, is chock-full of dust-catching, sentimental bric-a-brac which you imagine will be useful or valuable one day, know that your mind is in the grip of poverty consciousness.

To counteract this tendency, train your mind to accept the abundant inner riches bestowed on you by God and lead a materially simple life, eschewing luxuries. Objects are temporarily on loan from the *dharma* field for our spiritual growth, and we should be willing to release them back to the field at a moment's notice.

As the story goes, the Buddha needed a job because he fell in love with a rich woman. So he went for an interview and, seeing that he was a monk, the employer asked about his qualifications, to which the Buddha replied, "I can wait, I can fast and I can think." He was hired on the spot. When you are experiencing the bliss of *sattva*, you are in no hurry to pursue objects. If you do, you purse them with dignity.

21. ABSENCE OF OWNERSHIP

This value is similar to absence of pride and absence of ego. Here is another clever analysis: Is the body mine? My mother can claim it, in that it is made out of her flesh. The father can claim it, in that it cannot come into being without his seed. It cannot survive without parents to take care of it. The family has a claim, the society too, the bank that keeps your money safe, for instance. Myriad creatures, including bacteria of all ilk, air, fire, water and earth, the sun and moon and so on all have a claim. At best I am a trustee or a tourist taking up temporary residence as the *karma* for this incarnation plays out.

Without the idea of ownership my relationship with objects becomes purely factual, and in the absence of attachment my mind becomes settled and capable of inquiry. *Isvara* owns it all. Two positive values that correspond with absence of ownership are charity and generosity. The heart that gives gathers.

22. LOVE OF SOLITUDE

Love of solitude is an obviously valuable value, as one cannot inquire when the mind is connected to and surrounded by other busy minds. Love of solitude is not escapism, because the need to escape indicates an inability to face oneself. An activity that leaves you feeling incomplete when you cannot do it has become an escape. Love of solitude is a mind that enjoys being with itself and is the perfect environment for self-inquiry.

23. RESOLUTION, COMPLETION

Excessive *rajas* is the bane of spiritual life. While individuals with *tamasic* minds find it difficult to initiate projects, individuals with scattered *rajasic* minds find it difficult not to start projects and equally difficult to complete them. Unless you follow through on a resolution, your mind will become more and more disturbed as unfulfilled tendencies build up. So it is necessary to have a strong value for completing actions. To master this value, do one thing at a time – no multitasking! Only when a given project is completed do I take up the next. In addition to *karma yoga*, it is necessary to identify the source of my many activities as a false idea of who I am and neutralize it with the knowledge "I am whole and complete." Nothing that I do will change who I am. And once I am committed to liberation and understand the value of inquiry, I must stick to my practice until I am free.

24. APPRECIATION OF TIME

This value is little more than looking at the downside of the very process of life itself. Birth is wonderful perhaps, but it ceases to be so wonderful when you consider death. And the space between birth and death is no bed of roses either; we are all treated to various physical and psychological pains daily.

Today you may be happy, but tomorrow you may suffer. Time is a ravenous mouth, consuming everything, including pain. Nothing can be done about it, so keep your goal in mind. Don't fritter it away. Become a master of time and hasten slowly.

25. SERVICE TO THE TEACHER

Service to the teacher should not be given lightly and only to a teacher of great integrity who does not ask for it, because he or she has no need for it. A teacher who demands surrender is not a true teacher, and the misguided student who surrenders to such a person is asking for suffering. When I asked my teacher how I could serve him, he said, "Keeping one's mind on *Isvara* is the only service."

Service is a state of mind that does not require physical action, only the willingness to act. In the ideal student-teacher relationship there is no give-and-take as in other relationships.

There is only giving on the part of the student. The teacher is a stand-in for the Self and serves by providing an object of meditation, not adulation. If the teacher is established in the Self as the Self and has worked out all personal issues, the opportunity to serve a teacher is the greatest blessing.

26. COMPASSION ~ FORGIVENESS

Compassion is empathy, a natural, active expression of love and should not be suppressed. Because a *sattvic* mind sees the *dharma* field clearly and knows the power of binding *vasanas,* it appreciates the fact that nobody breaks *dharma* if they can help it, so it inclines the *jiva* to forgiveness.

27. HUMILITY

Humility is born of an appreciation of the glory of *Isvara* and the non-difference of all beings.

28. MODESTY

Modesty is unpretentiousness caused by the knowledge that whatever talents and abilities I possess are due to *Isvara's* grace alone.

29. FORBEARANCE

Non-complaining acceptance of unconducive circumstances without seeking redress or revenge is forbearance.

Non-Conforming Values to Be Removed

Tamasic and *rajasic* impediments are: anger, lust, greed, lack of discrimination between right and wrong, cruelty, conceit, vanity, pretentiousness, the tendency to attribute bad qualities to good people, self-pity, desire for sense enjoyment, envy, hatred, obsessiveness, attempting to prosper at the expense of others, gossip, regret after giving, suffering humiliation out of a desire for a petty gain, failure to exercise discrimination when you know what it is, inflating your good or bad qualities, refusing to acknowledge your good or bad qualities and treating those who are dependent on you as inferiors.

1. GRATUITOUS DESIRES AND FEARS

Desire is not necessarily your enemy. Where desire is absent, death is present. Desire channeled toward noble ends is scripturally sanctioned. Frivolous, unnecessary desires are not sanctioned and need to be removed.

Fear in the form of prudent caution is sanctioned, but not at the expense of trust in the benign, non-dual nature of reality. Trust the Lord and tether your camel. When your life is in danger, fear is eminently reasonable. Fear that you can't get a reservation at your favorite restaurant indicates skewed priorities.

2. UNJUSTIFIED ANGER

Anger, obstructed desire, is generally a useless emotion, indicating attachment to petty, worldly things. However, anger generated by violations of *dharma* is justified insofar as it leads to punishment of perpetrators. If the rules of the *dharma* field are unenforced, society becomes chaotic and purposeful work is not possible. If you are not critical of yourself for your bad values, you have normalized the abnormal. Legitimate self-disgust should motivate a commitment to work on yourself, not harden into a permanent self-negating scowl.

3. DELUSION

Delusion is the belief that happiness depends on getting what you want and avoiding what you don't want. Because it is hardwired, it is difficult to objectify and extremely difficult to remove. Delusion is the "normal" human state of mind.

4. STINGINESS, MISERLINESS

A failure to appreciate the generous fullness of life, stinginess is an ugly emotion born of a false sense of smallness and lack.

5. ARROGANCE

Arrogance is an unconscious emotion generated out of an extremely low sense of self-worth, an attempt by an insecure person to elevate his or her status at the expense of others.

6. COMPARISON

Comparison is the first manifestation of duality and leads to competitiveness, status-consciousness, jealousy, envy and *schadenfreude*.

Rather than compare yourself to others, you should evaluate yourself with reference to your progress toward maintaining a simple, uncluttered mind.

7. THE NEED TO CONTROL

The need to control is a futile, fear-oriented value, indicating extremely low self-esteem. All beings follow their natures; what use is control?

8. GUILT AND REGRET

Guilt and regret are nasty thoughts that point to transgressions of universal values and/or inauthenticity caused by a refusal to accept your relative nature. The desire to be different is the scourge of the modern era. Yes, perhaps you do need a bit of work, but you cannot change yourself without first accepting yourself as you are, warts and all.

If I refuse to own these feelings, I can address the value that caused the transgression. Here is a *mantra* that should be chanted when these feelings arise: "Desire does it. Desire is the doer. I am not the doer. Desire causes action. I do not cause action. Salutations to you, Desire. Anger does it. I don't do it. My prostrations to you, Anger. Ignorance caused it. I am not ignorant. Obeisance to you, O Ignorance." Fear-oriented individuals can substitute the word "fear" for "desire."

9. JEALOUSY AND ENVY

A common and unreasonable impurity born of a sense of lack, jealousy is a pernicious form of duality. It exists because the world is filled with millions of entities that provide myriad opportunities, real or imagined, for self-demeaning, comparative judgments. Jealousy and envy are transformed anger and usually lead to depression.

Here is an easy, factual way to neutralize these feelings: there is only one Self and everyone is it, so no one is superior or inferior. But if this is too simple, here is another inquiry that should lay them to rest: I am never jealous of the whole person, only some aspect. There are certain things about him that I don't want, just as I too have unattractive qualities, which makes it difficult to judge him. The fact that I would like to be like him shows that there is some sympathy for him. How can I separate the bad qualities from the whole person? Because the complete person can never be an object of envy, there is no place for my bad feelings to attach.

Jealousy is due to an insufficient appreciation of my own nature and the abundance of good qualities that spring from it. When I feel jealousy, I should apply the opposite thought and nip it in the bud, lest it devolve into a seriously *tamasic* and truly despicable emotion, *schadenfreude,* delight in the misery of others. I should think, "I am happy for the good fortune of this person. I admire his good qualities. I am happy that he is happy."

10. Pride, Vanity, Conceit, Self-Glorification

A simple, factual, *sattvic* self-respect is a good quality. However, most of us have doubts about our adequacy (*tamas*). We secretly fear that we are not good enough and are unable to provide ourselves with the confidence we need to be happy, so we look to others to validate us. To gain validation we are often tempted to exaggerate our qualifications and accomplishments so that others will think we are special and glorify us. If I am completely certain about my talents and abilities, I take them for granted and have no need for validation or support.

Demanding respect from others invites many disturbances because the one who asks for respect is not in control of the result. People give it for reasons known only to them. When their minds change, the validation is withdrawn and hurt arises. Any form of hurt is due to pride, an inflated ego, one that is excessively attached to what it thinks it knows, believes or possesses. For example, individuals who spend an inordinate amount of time grooming and calling attention to their bodies with expensive clothing, outlandish hairdos, tattoos and piercings, usually do so to attract attention they are incapable of giving themselves. Such egos, inflated by pride and vanity, invariably end up deflated. Often they waste time and energy trying to save face or plotting revenge. Additionally, it is not always easy to determine another person's true feelings.

A person who lives by the opinions of others squanders valuable mental resources and is not qualified for inquiry.

The Solution: Inquiry into Isvara

If I take time to analyze the factors involved, I will clearly see that demanding respect from others cannot bring comfort or satisfaction, even if I am a highly accomplished person. First, I should investigate the basis of the factors that motivate me to demand respect from the world. The answer is that I believe that I am the author of my actions, the producer and owner of my gifts and skills. But is this true? What did I actually create? It is clear that I did not create my body.

I appeared here one fine day encased in a fleshy meat tube by no effort of my own. I did not create my sense of individuality either: it came along with the body and the world in which the body exists, a world that I definitely did not create. Certain skills and abilities sprouted from within me by no will of my own. I can utilize them, but I cannot claim authorship of them. Whatever achievements I claim depended on opportunities that were provided by life itself. I did not cook them up. I just happened to be in the right place at the right time. How I got there is a mystery.

If I am a reasonable person, I should conclude that the gifts I enjoy speak for themselves. Whether or not they are noticed and appreciated by others should not concern me. A flower in a vacant slum lot blooms unnoticed for no other reason than it is its nature to bloom. Pride can fall away when I see that it is a false value that impedes growth.

11. Pretension, Affectation, Lying

Pride is based on real accomplishments or abilities, but pretension is self-glorification without cause. I want to give the impression that I am something I am not. If I dress like a prince, my bank account is overdrawn and I am dodging bill collectors, I am pretentious. If I claim to have a country estate in the South of France when I live in a rent-controlled apartment in a ghetto, I am pretentious. If I can't answer the doorbell without first tidying the living room for fear that someone might think I am a messy person or I cannot appear in public in a mismatched outfit without my lipstick and every hair in place, I am a poseur. If I have done no meaningful spiritual work but wear orange robes, shave my head, carry a staff and wander from one spiritual center to another with a beatific smile pasted on my face to convince others of my mystic attainments, I am not a *mahatma*. I am a phony.

Affectation is a particularly difficult problem because I don't even have the satisfaction of knowing that what I am saying about myself is true. I am therefore committed to falsehood. This attitude is particularly vexatious because there is no way to compel others to respond favorably to my lies. Because I badly need a response and because at any time my lie may be exposed, I am subjected to a surfeit of stress. To make it work I need to be very alert, keep all my friends apart and have a very long memory.

There is a belief that the *karma yoga* attitude – leaving the result to *Isvara* – works in this situation, but it doesn't, because *karma yoga* is right action too, which assumes that one's values are in order. The *karma yoga* attitude should not be used to mask psychological problems or manage *adharmic* situations.

The solution is to admit the problem, accept scripture's idea of who I am and be willing to consider others' views because they see what I don't see about myself. Or I should have the confidence to discount their views because I know that they are projecting a false image onto me owing to their own lack of clarity. There is no learning and no growth for poseurs. I cannot solve even the basic problems of desire and anger if I am a proud, pretentious person. Without it I can become a clean, simple individual capable of honest self-examination.

Implementation of Values

Common sense is the first victim of material success. Because we don't really have to worry about food and shelter these days, we can afford to be lazy, stupid and ideological. When ex-president Clinton was asked why he got sexually involved with a White House intern, he replied, "Because I could." Because you can, a fine example of *rajas*-think, is not a legitimate reason to do anything. If you want to be happy, your actions should be *sattvic*, i.e. timely and appropriate to your nature and your station in life. His actions would not have created unwanted *karma* for him if he had waited until he was unmarried and out of office before he got entangled.

A bit of *tamas* might have served him well because he may not have noticed that Monica was making eyes at him. If you were fortunate enough to have been raised in a cultivated, sensible family, the following values will be second nature, but if not you need to appreciate the value of values and daily cultivate those conducive to inquiry. The mind is not going to roll over and play dead just to please you, like your darling dog Fido. Values are as values do. Here is a list of *sattvic* values required to implement the qualifying values listed above.

1. Resolve, Discipline, Autosuggestion

Discipline is a beneficial use of *rajas,* as it removes *tamas* and generates *sattva.* Physical discipline is *sattvic* eating, developing adequate *tamas* for sufficient sleep and regular exercise. Mental discipline, making resolutions and sticking with them, is a *sattvic* use of *rajas* and *tamas.*

Verbal non-injury is one of the most overlooked values. Words are extremely powerful; a single inadvertent use of an ill-considered unedited sentence can instantly turn good *karma* into bad *karma.* Make a resolution to monitor the content of your speech and your tone of voice. Most of us are not aware of the implied meaning of our words or the impact of our tone of voice. Think about what you want to say and how you want to say it before you speak. People will listen if it is obvious that you have taken care to get your thoughts in order before you speak.

Make a resolution to stop gossiping. Studies indicate that sixty-five percent of human speech is gossip. It is sign of low self-esteem, insofar as criticizing or putting someone down is a cowardly way to make yourself feel better, not to mention a complete waste of time. Make a resolution not to argue. Don't offer an opinion unless it is solicited. Nobody really cares what you think.

Talking to a person who does not want to listen is violence. Speaking harshly, contemptuously and cynically is violence. Speaking uncontrollably without letting the other person get a word in edgewise is *rajasic.* Speaking without considering the context is *tamasic.* Speaking in short sentences, paying attention to how the words are received, with the idea of learning what the recipient thinks, is *sattvic* and creates favorable opportunities. Saying more than necessary just to hear the sound of your own voice is *rajasic.* Interrupting when someone is speaking is *rajasic.* Speaking the truth in a beneficial, pleasant, polite, gentle or humorous way without hurting the recipient's feelings is *sattvic.* The need to say something that the recipient does not want to hear is *rajasic/ tamasic.* Offering unsolicited advice is *rajasic/tamasic.*

If you are miserly and possessive – your house is cluttered with bric-a-brac – make a resolution to give something away every day – your time, money, unnecessary possessions, etc. Determine to read scripture for thirty minutes every day and stubbornly (*tamas*) stick to it. Remain concentrated on your chosen value for a month and observe the beneficial results.

2. Precaution

Prudence is a *sattvic* use of fear. It prevents dread, crippling *tamas.* That things go wrong is a fact of life. Assuming that they won't is foolish. Be prudent. There is no need to worry if you have your ducks in line before you rush out to face the day.

I once read a statistic that Americans spend 1.6 years of their lives looking for lost objects, presumably because their minds are scattered and they are swimming in an ocean of poorly organized things. Resolve to remain mindful when you pick up an object (no grabbing!) or release an object from your grasp.

Rajas forces attention ahead of itself. Thoughts precede actions. Attention should be synchronized with the thought associated with the action happening in the moment, not running ahead to the next thought before the action is completed. When you come home after a hard day at the office, primed with a long list of household chores that you believe need to happen before you can sleep, and the phone rings, don't just frantically grab it for fear of missing the call. Let it ring until you have consciously placed the keys where they belong. If you answer the phone with the keys still in hand and wander outside to turn on the sprinkler as you chat, you will unconsciously put them on the garden table so you can turn on the water. When you need them the last place you will look is the garden table. If you're treated to a disapproving look from the boss when you arrive late at the office with a sheepish grin on you face, you have only yourself to blame. Show up late one time too many because you are too disorganized to use common sense, and you may be looking for another job.

3, 4. RESTRAINT, INTROSPECTION

Tamas inclines one to avoidance. Avoiding necessary and uplifting activities is a poor use of this energy, but avoiding self-defeating habits is beneficial. For instance, you can avoid a life of self-imposed poverty by keeping a list of every dollar you spend every day, review (introspection) the list every evening, tick-mark unnecessary purchases, keep a separate tally of them and review it every month. Luxuries have a way of becoming necessities.

If you feel the need to treat yourself to frivolous things, your self-esteem is very low because you are being controlled by your desires. If you hear yourself justifying an unnecessary purchase with the words, "It was on sale. I saved ten dollars," or, "I deserve it," you have been totally brainwashed by the business community. You don't realize that it is standard practice in the retail trade to quadruple the cost of new items to grab the money of early adopters, needy types, and cut it in half two weeks later so the business merely doubles its money. You didn't actually save a dime. The savings were all in your mind, not in your bank account. You spent ten dollars. Take an honest inventory of your values and vow to avoid waste.

Treat yourself to a dose of willpower and feel good about yourself. When you resolve to tackle wastefulness, your worries will start to abate. Three dollars for a latte seems like nothing when you spend it. Just say no and have a drink of water. Forgo the inevitable impulse buys at the supermarket checkout – you do not need to know why Brad and Angelina are getting a divorce – add to your coffee savings and get a round-trip ticket to a Caribbean island at the end of the year to get a bit of relief from your petty, boring, self-indulgent life. Or, heaven forbid, ask why you need to escape in the first place. If you were okay with yourself, you might even be comfortable donating your latte savings to your favorite charity and pick up some good *karma*.

Overcoming bad values is not easy. *Rajas* and *tamas* constantly chip away at your resolve. It's a shame that penance, a productive use of *rajas/tamas,* has gone out of fashion. In the good old days when people had a bit of moral fiber, they would wear the hair shirt until their transgressions were firmly etched in memory rather than wait to be clapped in the stocks. Obviously, the cat-o'-nine-tails and thumb screws are not going to make a comeback, but you should introduce some version of the dunce cap to keep yourself on track.

When you transgress a value to which you are committed, commit yourself to mindfully repeating, "I am whole and complete, limitless bliss/consciousness," one hundred times. Writing is even better. Or sincerely repeat a general prayer for the well-being of others one hundred times. If you have a problem acknowledging others' accomplishments, apply the opposite value by daily looking for opportunities to praise someone. It may seem silly or childish, but you wouldn't need to do it if you were spiritually mature.

5. Prayer

Here are Swami Paramarthananda's rules of prayer: "Nobody fails to benefit from God's grace. In fact the life that we value so much is God's grace, but this does not absolve us of the responsibility to work on ourselves. Nor should we arrogantly believe that we can accomplish everything on our own. Pride goes before a fall. We should appreciate our role and the role of *Isvara* by taking responsibility and seeking *Isvara's* grace through prayer.

"Know what to ask for. It is important to understand that while *Isvara*, the Creator, is omnipotent, it is not going to suspend the fundamental rules of existence to satisfy frivolous desires. Omnipotence is not the capacity to do anything. It is the capacity to do everything that is possible in a given context. Therefore don't pray to escape change, particularly death. It may have escaped your attention, but change is non-negotiable. Pray for what is possible.

"As long as we live, we have to be physically and mentally active, so asking to be relieved of the responsibility to act is useless. Neglect is a sin. If you have children, you must look after them. Escapism is a sin. If you drop out of society to become a wandering monk, you will never have a moment's rest. But you can pray for freedom from subjective problems, like boredom, the scourge of our age. Here is a good prayer: 'O Lord, let me act every moment with a cheerful mind. Give me the inspiration to do what I need to do.'

"The future is never under our control, so any prayer that involves an attempt to control the future will fail miserably. You cannot make your children achieve what you want them to achieve, only God can. But you can enthusiastically contribute to their growth so that they will find success in accordance with their natures.

"Wanting people to be different is an impossible prayer. Every person follows his or her own nature without fail, what use is control? Praying for individuals and the world to conform to your idea is useless and frustrating. Encouraging others to follow their God-given natures and grow into the light is a useful prayer. 'O Lord, let me live in such a way that my life is an inspiration to others' is a reasonable prayer. 'O Lord, make me aware of my judgmental thoughts and grant me the ability to accommodate others. Let me speak with kindness,' is another.

"None of us is satisfied with ourselves, but wanting yourself to be different is also an impossible prayer. Even God cannot change you, because what you are is the result of your actions. You will never become someone else. It is useless to judge yourself and refuse to accommodate to what you are at any given moment. We can only grow according to God's idea. So the prayer should be: 'Grant me the dispassion to accept myself as I am and the discrimination to do what is right in every moment, irrespective of how I feel.'

"Life is a set-up. We can never get total satisfaction and security through a set-up. Praying for an ideal situation is a pipe dream. Even ideal set-ups become upsets. 'O Lord, let me discover security and satisfaction in myself, whatever the circumstances.'

"It is natural to complain. Even *Isvara's* complaints are justified. It created the world, created all beings and gave us a set of rules called *dharma* that we are expected to follow. And what do we do? We violate every rule in the book! But complaining is a bad feeling that gets us nothing but more bad feelings. Praying for the right things in the right spirit is uplifting. You feel good about yourself when you pray. It is the best vehicle for growth.

An Excellent Prayer

"'O Lord, let me be cheerfully and enthusiastically active. Let me enjoy whatever I do. Let me contribute to the future; let me not try to control it. Let me influence others positively through my life and language; let me not try to change others. Let me have the wisdom to discover satisfaction and security within myself, whatever be the set-up.' If we pray in this way, God will certainly cooperate."

6. Monitor States of Mind, and Think the Guna Through

Gunas are global values; thoughts and feelings are local values. You needn't waste a lot of time analyzing the meaning of specific thoughts and feelings if you can identify the *guna* with which a thought or feeling is associated. The law of *karma* dictates the results of your actions. If acting out of *rajoguna* produces predictably unwanted results in a particular situation, switch to *sattvaguna* the next time the situation occurs. For instance, you encounter problems whenever you relate to a particularly competent and valuable subordinate because a *tamasic* sense of insecurity invokes *rajas* and causes you to assert your dominance when you interact. Invoke *sattva* by relating as a friend the next time you meet and see if your relationship doesn't get more comfortable.

7. Apply the Opposite Energy

Yes, thought itself is hardwired, but individual thoughts are not, so it is eminently possible to deliberately create healthy thoughts and thought patterns. You don't have to discover the thoughts you need by going deep within and searching for them; Vedanta is a complete dictionary of healthy thoughts and thought patterns. As we have mentioned, duality means that every negative thought has a corresponding positive thought. So cancel a negative thought by applying its opposite.

Neutralize a stingy mind by giving generously. Neutralize a distrusting mind with a trusting mind. Wipe away a dirty thought with a clean thought, a depressing thought with an uplifting thought. "I am small and incomplete" is a negative thought. "I am whole and complete" is a positive thought.

8. Associate with Great Souls

Many Vedantic texts categorically say that association with great souls is the root cause of liberation. A great soul is not necessarily a fully self-actualized human, as these are very rare.

A great soul is any cultured person committed to higher values who is devoted to the Lord. Such associations are profound, incomprehensible, indescribable and will invariably convert a worldly person into a devotee, an atheist into a theist, a spiritual materialist into an inquirer, and an inquirer into a wise, non-dual devotee.

Seeking them rarely works because contact depends on an exceptional store of merit. Therefore may you be blessed with an association with a wise person who follows the *Upanishadic* tradition because Vedanta puts you in the driver's seat; it transfers a systematic methodology capable of removing self-ignorance to you. Because seekers are unclear about the nature of liberation, they don't know how to seek. If they knew what enlightenment was they wouldn't be seeking in the first place, so they are generally incapable of determining whether or not a teacher is the real thing. Therefore all you can do is pray.

How can we lump the grace of *Isvara* and the grace of *mahatmas* together? Because *mahatmas* have the firm knowledge that *Isvara* is their very essence. Even *mahatmas* who have dualistic devotion invoke *Isvara* at all times. If you worship such a *mahatma* the worship goes on to *Isvara*; it never remains with the teacher.

Meditation

A. Dual and Non-Dual

The popular view is that meditation is a technique that rids the mind of *rajas* and *tamas,* and invokes the experience of *sattva*, peace. It does not require Vedanta. So far we have presented meditation as *guna*-knowledge. Meditation with *guna*-knowledge is superior to therapeutic meditation because knowledge transforms the basic structure of the mind, whereas meditating for experience leaves the structure untouched and only momentarily quiets the surface, producing pleasant experiences.

Meditation is not for self-knowledge. If it were, there would be no need for Vedanta. Self-knowledge is communicated by a competent, living teacher unfolding a proven means of self-knowledge, and is a three-stage process: listening, reasoning and assimilation. Experience will not shift one's identity from the *jiva* to awareness, except perhaps temporarily. Meditators take the *jiva* to be the Self and want to give it a special experience. The practice of self-knowledge, which may be done in a meditative state or not, is required to completely shift the meaning of the word "I" from the *jiva* to consciousness. Vedantic meditation is for the assimilation of self-knowledge.

God's grace or a *guru's* grace are required for meditation, but both are useless unless you grace yourself with self-effort. The three limbs of your subtle body should be yoked to a single idea – liberation. The body should be healthy;

karma yoga should be converting your emotions into devotion and your thinking should be in harmony with scripture. Meditation is a disciplined activity that requires an appropriate ambience and a mediation-friendly posture wherein the body is properly aligned, the sense organs are withdrawn, the breathing is rhythmic, the emotions *sattvic* and a strong conviction that meditation is valuable is present.

Meditation is not removing thoughts. It is mentally dwelling on the many features of the Self – its non-duality, all-pervasiveness, timelessness, self-luminosity, independence, etc. and dwelling on the nature of objects, specifically their impermanence, the zero-sum nature of the world, doership, enjoyership and so on. It leads to complete absorption in the teaching.

The purpose is to create such a strong *satya-mithya vasana* that the knowledge is at your fingertips all day long. It is successful when dualistic thinking does not displace non-dual thought. Dualistic thinking may exist, but it is always subordinate to non-dual thought. The benefit is non-dual vision, unconditional self-love, compassion for all sentient beings. The obstacles are the usual suspects: *rajas* and *tamas*.

B. MINDFULNESS, BURNING DESIRE

The goal of inquiry, steady enjoyment of the blissful fullness of my nature, and the means, mindfulness, are similar. When, with the aid of the teaching, the knowledge of my desireless fullness is unshakable, the unchanging experience of my limitlessness requires no maintenance; I have transcended the *gunas* and experience fullness irrespective of my state of mind. But to get there, which is not actually a destination, I need mindfulness. Mindfulness is a state of intense concentration on the goal – freedom – brought about by a burning desire to be unshackled from objects.

An object is anything other than the *guna*-free Self: the body, mind and emotions, discrete experiences – activities, for instance – and the experience of physical objects. To be free of objects is not the experience of a life-denying void, one of the many fears encountered by spiritual seekers. On the contrary, the Self is limitless bliss, the essence of experience. And since the immortal Self is ever-present and you are non-separate from it, *guna* transcendence is tantamount to limitless bliss.

Nothing is accomplished without desire. Yet desire for objects scatters the mind of a worldly person, whereas it concentrates the mind on the Self of dedicated inquirers because they know that objects deliver as much pain as pleasure. Success in any endeavor requires concentration, from tying one's shoelaces to winning the presidency. So if the desire for freedom, the appreciation of the effortless, ever-present fullness of the one subject subsumes the desire for objects, and the subject is known to be free, either as a result of non-dual epiphanies or full faith in the words of the scripture, which categorically and endlessly claims that the subject is eternally full and free, the mind will remain concentrated, which is to say mindful, more or less constantly.

Unlike the tepid "mindfulness" teachings on offer in the spiritual market-place, which attempt to synchronize the mind with "the power of now," a sad proxy for the Self, and produce fleeting peaceful *sattvic* moments, intense passionate desire for liberation ironically produces the sustained, concentrated *sattva* known as *samadhi*, required for successful inquiry. So mindfulness is keeping the goal in mind. Keeping the goal in mind is difficult if there are other priorities, and easy if *guna* transcendence is the only priority.

Sublimation

So *guna* management is elimination of object-oriented desire by sublimating it into an all-consuming desire for freedom. *Guna* management requires an enlightened, *sattvic* lifestyle. An enlightened lifestyle is a scripturally sanctioned lifestyle, one in which all activities are directly or indirectly related to the desire to be free of the push and pull of objects. Freedom is not freedom from objects, which is only attained when you die. It is freedom from *samsara*, the belief that objects can complete you. *Karma yoga* and *jnana yoga*, Vedantic inquiry, are the two pillars on which an enlightened life rests.

Non-dual epiphanies brought about by the presence of dominant *sattva* will certainly produce the *rajas* necessary to temporarily concentrate the mind on the Self, but without a proper means of self-knowledge they usually become a goal in themselves, whereas they are simply one of many discrete, albeit sublime, *samsaric* experiences. Pain (*rajas*) caused by the unsuccessful pursuit of objects – particularly love – may also concentrate the mind and produce the sustained state of mind necessary for inquiry. Failure to succeed in the world should be counted as a blessing, a gift of disappointment, not evidence of low self-worth, because worldly success is subject to the usual downsides.

But what about a person who has a pleasant enough life and has not been blessed – or cursed, as the case may be – with a non-dual epiphany or with the purifying effects of failure?

Trust Dissatisfaction ~ Stuck in Sattva

Unless you know who you are in the form of the palpable, ever-present, *guna*-free experience of unconditional love, you are dissatisfied in one way or another. The attainment of *samsaric* goals – the trophy spouse, wealth, fame, power, knowledge, etc. – are never enough. If you are stuck in worldly success, you need to trust that niggling, ever-present and difficult-to-acknowledge sense of dissatisfaction that trails you constantly like a needy little dog. It does not go away, no matter how much you have accomplished. It is the desire for freedom born of the presence of the Self, enticing you to inquire. Feed it. Use whatever energy is left in your short life to commit yourself to inquiry, and follow the program.

No Magic Formula

Most humans are *tamasic*; they love formulas. If you have a nice formula like Colonel Sanders' secret blend of eleven herbs and spices, you only need to apply it mindlessly over and over to get rich selling scads of dead chickens.

Unfortunately, there is no simple *guna* formula for successful inquiry: mix two parts *rajas*, three parts *sattva* and one part *tamas* on Monday, three parts *rajas*, two parts *sattva* and two parts *tamas* on Tuesday, throw in a pinch of pure consciousness – and *voilà!* – a successful life.

Why? Because the *gunas* modifying your primary instrument are in a state of constant flux, meaning your mind and emotions are constantly changing, and your environment, meaning *Isvara*, is in a state of constant flux. Getting the right subjective *guna* to appear at the right time to satisfy the *guna* demand of the field at any moment, particularly when you are burdened with the vanity that your needs trump the needs of the field, counts as luck, not a *guna*-managed life.

The Right Formula

The right formula is keeping your goal in mind at all times and following the program outlined in this book. If you don't manage your *gunas*, they simply default to their ignorance-motivated setting and inflict misery on you.

Mindfulness is paying attention to the *guna* at play in the moment and making the required adjustment, should one be required. In the case of inquiry, the *gunas* need to be balanced in this way: (1) sufficient *tamas* to put the knowledge gained from inquiry into practice and to sleep six to eight hours a day, (2) sufficient *rajas* to overcome *tamasic* habits and to actively pursue self-inquiry *à la* Vedanta and (3) sufficient *sattva* to keep the mind clear enough to discriminate the Self from the *gunas* and keep *rajasic* projections to a minimum.

Observe and Adjust

When I was young, I was a committed materialist. Among other things, sex and money, for instance, I was a glutton specializing in red meat and alcohol. In time

I puffed up like a balloon, became quite dull and found my energy flagging. So I took the bull by the horns, cut back on the quantity and changed the quality of my food. I read a few books on healthy eating, quit red meat (*tamas*) and took to fried chicken, which is more *sattvic* than beef but still *tamasic* overall.

In a few weeks I felt lighter and experienced increased energy. But after a month or so I started to feel *tamasic* again, so I quit frying the chicken, cut off the fat, started broiling the flesh and experienced lightness and increased energy. Eventually *tamas* showed up like a bad penny. I knew better than to fry it, because hot oil is *tamasic*, so I switched to grilled fish because it is more *sattvic* than chicken, owing to the fact that it is a water creature, not a land animal.

Each time I adjusted my food source, the *tamas* was less *tamasic* because it was mixed with more *sattva,* and less frequent because there was less of it overall. The war of the *gunas* continued, so I moved from fish to vegetarian macrobiotics. If veganism had been around, I probably would have given it a try. Fruitarianism was an option, but I was *sattvic* and *rajasic* enough by that time. Had I become a fruitarian and found it lacking, the blissful glories of breatharianism waited. After that, the only option is death because you can't get rid of any *guna* completely.

I met a few people who claimed they lived on the energy in the air. Perhaps they did, but it did not generate interest in that way of life insofar as their minds were so dull they were essentially useless. In any case, after a year or so I was lean, fit and brimming with *rajas* and *sattva*. A few years down the line I got so *sattvic* I hardly slept, meditated most of the time and was "gone with the fairies," as they say. And the solution? Light meat with my veggies. Sleep returned and I could tie my shoelaces again.

The body belongs to the field, and as the field changes, what's *rajasic, tamasic* or *sattvic* today will not necessarily be *rajasic, tamasic* or *sattvic* tomorrow. And the moral of the story? Constant vigilance is the price of freedom because, although formulas may work, their shelf life is short.

Because there is no magic *guna* formula, you need to recognize the feeling, thought and value of each *guna* and discover their effects in various situations, keep your mind as *sattvic* as possible and apply the action that generates the appropriate *guna* on the fly so that your causal body delivers the appropriate thought/feeling/action to the subtle body next time. And you need to be a good *karma yogi* because you don't always get it right.

You Are Not What You Eat

Guna-knowledge works with every aspect of your life because every aspect of life is the three *gunas*. Humans are driven by a complex of subtle and gross-body instincts (*vasanas*) that need to be managed as they arise.

Experience involves three factors: pure original consciousness, reflected consciousness and thoughts, which produce emotions and actions. The thoughts arising in the reflection, the subtle body, are born of the *gunas* as they appear as our likes and dislikes. Likes – *rajas* – cause us to move toward objects, and dislikes – *tamas* – cause us to avoid objects. Life is mainly chasing things, avoiding things and dithering while we try to figure out which will produce the most pleasure and least pain. Mindfulness, the foundation of discrimination, is continually paying attention to these two tendencies.

Extroverted people are not mindful, because their minds are bewitched by their likes and dislikes. If you are not mindful, your thinking is purely mechanical. If you are mindful, you can evaluate your likes and dislikes, and consciously restrain from identifying with them, giving you remarkable control over your actions. If you don't take them as commands and don't pander to them, you are free to critically evaluate them with reference to your goals. Extroverts don't evaluate their *gunas,* because they are slaves to them.

C. INQUIRY

Any reasonably intelligent individual critically evaluates his likes and dislikes, since they cause good and bad *karma*. Wanting to escape bad *karma* is understandable, but why would I want to escape good *karma*? Because good *karma*, which is just events lining up with your likes, is not unconditional satisfaction since likes imply dislikes and since even *sattva* produces suffering, as it is in duality. However, as suffering goes, *sattva* is definitely superior to *rajas* and *tamas*.

Getting your desires more or less continually satisfied is not the kiss of death, obviously, but once you have achieved this state, you will become exceedingly bored, a type of privileged torment *Isvara* reserves for the successful. Boredom is nothing more than a desire for change.

In other words, you are bothered by *rajas*, but there is nowhere to go with it. So you find yourself trying to wring a little more pleasure out of objects that have already yielded as much pleasure as they can give. Ouch!

No Purifier Like Self-Knowledge

Karma yoga neutralizes likes and dislikes excited by worldly events, making it possible to discriminate the *gunas* from the Self. Self-inquiry neutralizes likes and dislikes as subtle *karma* before they have a chance to become actions and invoke a response from the field. It is simply understanding that likes and dis-

THE YOGA of the THREE ENERGIES

likes are a problem, not a solution. If you repeatedly renounce them in favor of peace of mind, they rapidly disappear, although it can be a struggle to let them go. When they no longer compel action, they are converted to preferences and you are *guna*-free because preferences are optional. Take them or leave them; it's all the same.

Maintaining discrimination is difficult because it exposes the ego, which does not want to lose control insofar as it is totally identified with its likes and dislikes, so it will do anything to distract the mind.

Emotional Management ~ Don't Express, Don't Suppress, Sublimate

If your mind is not subtle enough to manage the likes and dislikes that produce difficult emotions using self-inquiry, then *karma yoga* is required. You manage the emotions by reminding yourself that you are happy to be alive, that your life is a gift from life and that since life brought you here it has the responsibility of looking after you according to its idea of what you need. So you gladly accept what happens as life's blessing, which neutralizes your likes and dislikes and produces sustained spiritual growth.

This summary suggests that *karma yoga* is only useful when something happens that triggers an unpleasant emotion – anger, for instance. But events contrary to your desires are not always required to produce anger. Sometimes angry, *rajasic* thoughts arise spontaneously from the causal body. Anger is one of *rajas'* signature thoughts.

How do you deal with it? You don't prolong the anger by going into blame mode or see it as evidence of spiritual failure and allow it to collapse into a *tamasic* depression. You take it with a glad heart because you know it is life's way of helping you investigate and eliminate the cause. Actually, it is not correct to think that events take place "outside," away from your body, and that they cause emotions, although it seems that way. Because reality is non-dual, there is no inside and outside.

The anger is already in you because *rajoguna* is one of the three pillars of the psyche. The "outside event" reminds you of a similar situation in the past and invokes the anger that is already there in the causal body. Actually, events are value-neutral because they are generated by the law of *karma*; they don't mean anything apart from your interpretation of them. If three people die in an automobile accident witnessed by you and a dog, only you feel distressed. It means nothing to the dog, because it doesn't interpret its experience according to a predefined program like humans do, even though it witnessed the event. It is only a dog program, even though it has a subtle and gross body like we do.

So you can transform the emotion without too much thought by assuming that it is somehow useful and necessary or it wouldn't be happening and leave it at that or you can go one step further and investigate the idea that is causing it and train yourself to look at it objectively. You might think, "Tens of thousands of people die every day and I am not bothered. I didn't know those people, so why do I care? What use is the emotion since they are already dead? Everything is ordained by the *dharma* field according to the *karma* of each individual. I had no control over the situation, so why should I worry about it? It is only their bodies that died, the *Jiva* didn't die. Maybe they had miserable lives and *Isvara* is mercifully giving them the opportunity to start again in better circumstances."

No Guna Google

No database is big enough to reveal the appropriate *guna* response to every possible situation, so you will never be able to get on the internet and find out how to succeed in a given situation. It is enough to understand the basic principles by virtue of a few examples.

Before we discuss the *jiva's* direct experience of the *gunas* we need to revisit the idea of non-duality because the purpose of *guna* management is *guna* transcendence, meaning non-duality. Implicit in the discussion so far is the idea that reality is a duality and that the subject is a *jiva* operating in a world other than it. But the ultimate purpose of the *guna* teaching is to understand that the *jiva* is an object and you are the subject, the non-dual, *guna*-free Self.

Non-Duality

So why not just skip the *guna* business and go directly to non-duality? Because it is not possible if your intellect is predominately *tamasic* or *rajasic*. So you need to manage your life in such a way that your intellect detaches from the body-mind-sense complex and attaches to the Self in the form of non-dual knowledge. The intellect is your most valuable tool, but if it spends its days managing *samsaric* problems without *karma yoga* it becomes dull, like a knife used to cut hardwood.

Using it to generate *sattva* keeps it sharp and serviceable. A prepared mind easily understands non-duality. If you can follow the logic below and accept the conclusion readily, you will understand non-duality.

Non-duality means that there is only you, limitless existence/consciousness, which in turn means that all objects are you, but you are not an object.

If you have transcended the *gunas,* you can confidently state, "All *gunas* are in me. I am not in them." Non-duality means that Self alone is real and that the three-dimensional space-time world is not real. There is no physical, experiential way to prove this assertion, because the experiencing entity is one of myriad unreal, albeit conscious, objects that cannot experience anything beyond the range of its instruments of experience. The only access to understanding this statement is to allow the scripture to reveal the logic behind it.

"Not real" does not mean that the *jiva* doesn't seem to experience time and space. It certainly seems to, but when you analyze your experience carefully, you can't say that your mind, your instrument of experience, travels through the senses and passes through space until it confronts an object, then re-enters the mind through the senses to deliver the knowledge of the object to you. If this was how it happened, you would be without a mind for as long as the mind was out there gathering information! If perception happened that way, you would also be without the experience of the field in which the object existed. But that is impossible, because the field of experience is you, and you are never not present.

The World Is There Because I See It

This statement may be difficult to understand: in actuality the objects that we know though experience are generated by the senses, and the senses are generated by the mind. This means that I don't see the world because it is there. It means that the world is there because I see it. In other words, a projecting mechanism – *Maya* – is operating behind my subtle body that is generating the appearance of an objective world.

A companion science, elementary particle physics, points out that an analysis of the constituents of an object at any level of Creation leads us back to the point where it is impossible to identify the object as our senses perceive it, which implies that what we see is a construct of our senses. It is important to note that inference is a valid means of knowledge.

Here is how perception works from the point of view of the body. The mind receives stimuli from the senses and integrates them into thoughts, which represent the objects that appear to be away from us. As are the material objects, the senses are part of *Maya's* projection on the non-dimensional screen of awareness. In any case, if we include the body as one of the many objects in the world, it too is experienced as a thought in the mind, and when we realize this fact, the space-time continuum suddenly collapses. Obviously, it doesn't collapse physically, because it is only a projection, like a hologram. It "collapses" as a location other than you. The dimensional world is only present when it is an object of thought.

Where is your body when you are asleep or when you are thinking of something else? Unbeknownst to you, but known to *Isvara*, it occupies a tiny speck in limitless space. The body "collapses" because you are not thinking it. If you are thinking a tree-thought as a result of direct perception or memory, the tree exists as long as the thought remains, but when the mind takes the form of another thought, the tree disappears and you enjoy a different thought/experience. But you never experience anything away from your mind. It is your primary instrument of experience and knowledge.

When we refer to the mind as an instrument of experience, duality is present because the word "instrument" implies an agent, a conscious being wielding the instrument. So looking at reality from the point of the experiencing instrument is not freedom, non-dual knowledge. How do we get non-dual knowledge?

Resolve the Experiencing Instrument into You

Just as we resolved objects into thoughts, we resolve the knowing/experiencing instrument into its apparent cause. Here is the logic.

1. Objects don't exist without knowledge of them. As soon as you think of something, it is known. You know/experience the moon when you think of the moon, whether or not the "real" moon is present. If the moon is out, you do not go to the physical moon, gather information, assimilate it, return to your mind and know the moon. The thought of the moon is equal to the moon. Without a thought, where is the object? No duality there.

2. You cannot think a thought unless you are conscious. Thoughts don't think themselves, because they are inert. Thoughts are effects. Something caused them. They have mass and they move. They are thought by someone or something. That something is original pure consciousness via the agency of *Maya*, and that someone is reflected consciousness, the *jiva*, the two of which on analysis are non-separate. Thoughts are all-pervading, unchanging consciousness apparently moving owing to the power of *Maya*. They are like waves in an ocean. They are non-separate from consciousness just as both the ocean and its waves are water.

3. If there is no actual difference between the thought of an object and the object, and there is no difference between the thought and consciousness, there is no difference between objects and consciousness. Therefore the world is me, consciousness, but I am not the world.

This is the knowledge of someone who has transcended the *gunas*. You cannot just skip from your *guna*-driven, *samsaric* state of mind to this knowledge effortlessly. You need to develop discrimination first. Inquiry is discriminating between *gunas* and separating the *gunas* from the Self, which is free of the *gunas*. Likes and dislikes, which are different for every *jiva*, are just two ego-defined emotional evaluations of each *guna*.

In this chapter inquiry is looking into the cause of positive and negative emotions because the reasons you feel good or bad are seldom good reasons. For instance, if you enjoy *tamas*, which you do if you consume *tamasic* food and drink, associate with *tamasic* people and do *tamasic* work, your primary instrument will be unsuitable for inquiry.

Keeping in mind that you don't have one *guna* without the other two and that all three are operative in every person and in every situation, it is still helpful to isolate the three type of thoughts with reference to their effects. Scripture says: (1) *sattvic* thoughts are born of bliss, (2) *rajasic* thoughts produce actions and (3) *tamasic* thoughts produce inaction.

Satya and Mithya

Because reality is non-dual, there is no time, space or cause and effect. Everything that is apparently happening is happening simultaneously on apparently different levels. As the Self shines, the mind thinks, the emotions feel and the body acts. However, *Maya* makes it seem as if time, space and causation are real. Because we live in the *Maya* world, Vedanta uses concepts appropriate to *Maya* to lead us out.

So when we say, for instance, that thoughts "cause" emotions, we don't mean that in reality they are different, we mean that feelings and thoughts are just two ways of looking at the same thing, just as time and space are two ways of looking at the world. For instance, there is a wooden chair in front of you, and if you are asked what you see, you will say that you see a chair, even though you may just as truthfully have said that you see wood. The chair and the wood, which exist simultaneously in the same locus, are not separate.

So when we say that *sattvic* thoughts are "born of bliss" we mean that there is no difference between bliss and *sattva*, only an apparent difference. By the grace of *Isvara* the bliss of awareness appears as the *sattva*. But when you hear that they are "born" of bliss you are motivated to seek *sattva* because of the promise of bliss.

It doesn't take a lot of work to see the wood, because you are already seeing it. It just takes a few words to point out that your knowledge is only partially in harmony with your experience. You only say "chair" but you could just as well have said "wood." Or you could have said, "I see wood in the form of a chair," which is complete knowledge.

When you experience a feeling, you are also experiencing a thought. The thought is the "wood" of the feeling. So to solve an emotional problem you should not focus on the feeling, which is not amenable to knowledge, you should focus on the thought, which is.

This is a fancy way of saying that all emotional problems are thought problems. So if you want to feel good, think thoughts that "cause" good feelings. Inability to appreciate this truth accounts for the fact that the healing world, for instance, is like a permanent stay in the hospital. People do leave it, not because they are healed, but because they are cured of the idea that generating good feelings to get rid of bad feelings doesn't address the real issue – the thoughts producing the disease. If someone is lonely, and you hug them, the loneliness goes away momentarily but returns shortly after the hug ends. The real cause cannot be solved by an emotion. Only knowledge works.

We also say *rajasic* thoughts produce actions, which is to say that when you think you are a victim, you will be angry and depressed emotionally, and predictably unattractive words will come out of your mouth. And finally, we say *tamasic* thoughts produce inaction. When you are not doing what *Isvara* asks, you feel guilty because *Isvara* is your own consciousness and you are not doing what is right for yourself.

To imagine that Vedanta's attack on experiential enlightenment is an attack on experience itself is ridiculous. Experience is consciousness; what else could it be? Unfortunately, the *gunas* are objects, like the chair that takes your attention away from the wood. So we need a teaching that reveals the "wood" of your experience. Freedom is not an experience; it is your nature. Keeping in mind the fact that in reality there is no way to completely isolate each *guna*, let's discuss the salient characteristics of each.

When you have words – *sattva, rajas* and *tamas* – to identify your subjective experience, by implication your attention goes to the Self, which is bliss and which you are always experiencing, just as your attention goes to the wood when it is pointed out that you are experiencing wood primarily and a chair incidentally. So all this talk about *gunas* – experience – is calculated to get you to look at the context in which they appear, and the context is – surprise! – you: limitless, ordinary existence/awareness. As soon as your mind is locked on you, you experience the rock-solid bliss of your existence, and your thoughts dissolve into it.

Chapter IX

Three Primary Thoughts *and* Emotions

Sattva: Gateway to Non-Duality

IF YOU WILL recall, we said that *Isvara* is original pure consciousness plus *sattva*. In Christian traditions *Isvara* is called God, a word that probably once meant "good," not the good that is opposed to bad, but absolute good – what is always auspicious. It is always auspicious that we exist, that we are conscious and that our nature is bliss. It is virtually impossible to say a bad word about *sattva*, the reflecting, revealing power. It appears as the "mirror of matter" at the very beginning of Creation. It is called a mirror because it reflects existence-consciousness brightly. Everything good that we experience here on earth in these bodies inheres in *sattva* and is reflected in our subtle bodies.

Creation is a projection, like a dream; it doesn't take time. A dream is like a movie in that it isn't real, but dreams aren't slowly assembled like movies. They appear all at once and they end abruptly. You also can't say that any part of the dream is more or less important than any other part. Yes, when you set about to interpret the dream you may assign more value to one event than another, but from the dream's perspective every event is just dream stuff.

Sattva, rajas and *tamas* are the stuff of which the dream of life is made. All are only existence/consciousness appearing in three forms.

Furthermore, you can't really break down each aspect of each *guna* in reality, except for the purpose of understanding, because they have no aspects. They just are what they are, one seamless whole. At the same time, we think life is a myriad of discrete events unfolding in sequence, that each inert or conscious object is different and separate, and that each is defined solely by its form and particular characteristics. This atomistic view is not real. However, it seems real to us and we cannot just dismiss it willy-nilly with a breezy spiritual slogan like "it is all one." It is all one, but this knowledge is meaningless unless it is gained through patient investigation and analysis of every aspect of our experience to get a clear idea of our strengths and weaknesses and the tools that will burnish our strengths and ameliorate our weaknesses. With this in mind, the qualities of *sattva* are organized holistically, not hierarchically, keeping in mind that all are just different ways of looking at it and that each aspect is as valuable as every other aspect.

1. An Early Warning System

In the Creation sequence presented in Chapter III, you will recall that the first Creation stage was pure *sattva* uncontaminated by *rajas*. This teaching gives us a clue to one of the most wonderful aspects of the *sattva*, introversion. In the following stages, the pure *sattva* is apparently disturbed and muddied by *rajas* and *tamas* successively, which may convey the idea that the *sattva* degenerates. It doesn't, although it seems to. It is always pure. Instead, let's take up the superimposition metaphor, which presents reality as layers simultaneously imposed by *Maya*. Of course the idea of layers also implies duality, so we haven't gained much in terms of non-duality. But let's conceive of the relationship between *sattva* and *rajas/tamas* in this way: *rajas* and *tamas* overlaid on a *sattvic* base, like two coats of paint on a clean wood floor. When *rajas* and *tamas* are the predominant energies, they more or less obscure the *sattva*. They don't completely hide it, but they conceal it in different ways. At the behest of the macrocosmic *vasanas*, *rajas* deflects it to predetermined objects, and those objects consequently appear to be attractive because they "shine" in *sattva's* reflected light.

The mind becomes extroverted as it dwells on the glow and develops an attachment to the object, hiding the true source. *Tamas*, on the other hand, so clouds the mind that the *sattva* is mostly concealed and at best produces a dull glow. So it is legitimate to see the *yoga* of the *gunas* not as generating *sattva*, although it seems to, but as revealing it. As the *yoga* proceeds, the glow of the *sattva* brightens, and the mind slowly turns inward and loses interest in worldly things.

If your mind is predominantly *sattvic,* your life flows effortlessly around obstacles like water around big rocks in a river because the *sattva* alerts you to the warning signs that precede eruptions of *rajasic* energy. Situations are only difficult if you are not prepared for them. They start in the mind in the form of thought, and if you can think the thoughts through in light of the teachings, *rajas* does not have a chance to mature into deluding emotions that inevitably morph into *karmic* problems, conflict with others in particular.

2. Happiness

The self is bliss (*anandam*). It is not a bliss that you experience as a discrete feeling; it is the fullness, daresay the majesty, of existence itself. This bliss, reflected in the subtle body, the mind/heart, is experienced as happiness, satisfaction and peace. We have these words and others to describe it, but it is an extremely desirable, wordless experience. It is so valuable that nobody ever wants it to end, because it is based on an absolute value, the bliss of being. It does come and go, however, because no subtle body is one hundred percent *sattvic*. Consistent management for *sattva* can render the subtle body perhaps eighty percent *sattvic*. But *tamas* and *rajas* will have their day, not that either of them in small proportions are not useful or pleasant.

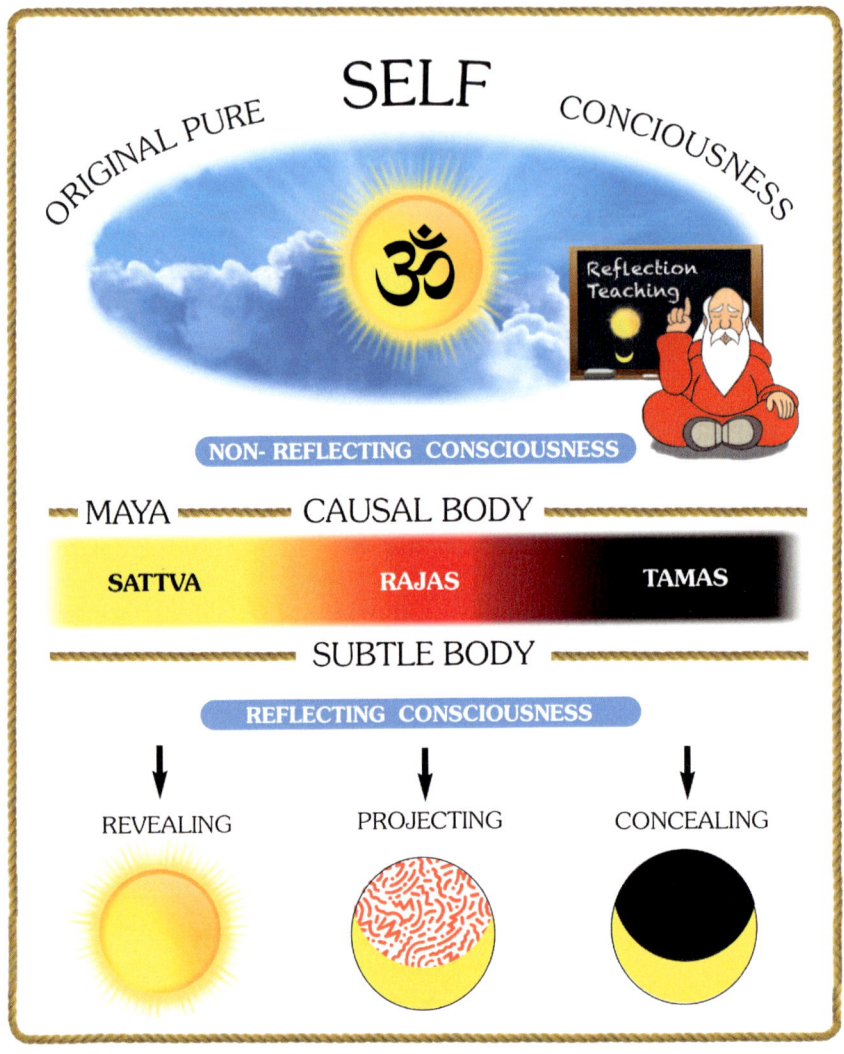

The immediate, palpable, direct, sustained experience of the *sattva* impacts the doer directly. It does not eliminate doership, but it changes the *jiva's* relationship to action. Whereas previously I did what I did for happiness, I now do what I do happily. The bliss of *sattva* is reflected in all my activities, and my life flows logically and effortlessly from one satisfying experience to the next. Yes, I am dynamic, but I am equally patient, skillful and confident. This limitless, partless fullness is experienced by the *jiva* as a sense of all-encompassing and gracious generosity of spirit.

No Direct Experience of the Self

When the modern spiritual teachers talk about "direct experience" of the Self or non-duality, they have mistaken *sattva* for *sat*, pure consciousness. You cannot directly or indirectly experience your Self, because you are your Self. Both words, "direct" and "indirect," imply duality. It is a seductive but cruel teaching because the poor seekers expect lasting bliss and end up with temporary bliss when the experiencing instrument is once again dominated by *rajas* or *tamas*. Non-duality means that you are always experiencing your Self because there is no other option.

3. LOVE, PLEASURE

Predominant *rajas* compels the *jiva* to action, and predominant *tamas* attracts the *jiva* to the heavy, narcotic pleasures afforded by the realm of the senses, but predominant *sattva* establishes the *jiva* in love. Consequently *sattvic* people are radiantly attractive. Because everyone loves love, many are willing to grease the wheels of life for them. Consequently owing to plentiful opportunities, someone established in *sattva* tends to be successful.

Because *sattva's* kindly face is turned toward the Self, unlike *tamas* and *rajas* who stare at the world though meaty, selfish eyes looking for physical loves or through sentimental eyes looking for romantic loves, *sattva* inclines the individual to a noble, lofty love. Unlike *rajasic/tamasic* individuals only interested in their own experiences, *sattvic* people are sympathetic and compassionate toward others.

A *rajasic/tamasic* doer-enjoyer believes that pleasure is inherent in objects and activities, while it actually resides in the *sattva*. When you get what you want or avoid what you don't, the *rajas* motivating your pursuit dissolves and the mind becomes momentarily *sattvic*, delivering reflected bliss to the *jiva*.

4. BEAUTY

There is no accounting for beauty from an individual perspective. An object is beautiful or ugly according to one's like and dislikes. But *sattva* reflects consciousness, the beauty that makes beauty beautiful. A purely *sattvic* mind sees beauty in everything.

5. FREEDOM

We could make the case that love of freedom should top the list of *sattvic* values insofar as Vedanta introduces itself with the contention that everything we do is an attempt to remove a sense of limitation. At the same time, we could argue that every action is an attempt to please the Self insofar as no one consciously does actions to displease themselves. Under the spell of this *guna*, the mind longs for freedom because the ever-free Self is witnessed clearly as a reflection in the *sattva*. It longs for political, social and existential freedom. It longs for freedom from want and ignorance, and it longs to be free of itself. The desire is always present because *sattva* is an indispensable component of the mind stuff, but it is more or less unknown when the mind is dominated by *rajas* and *tamas*.

6. Knowledge

Consciousness is the cause of knowledge. We don't know anything unless we are conscious. And the *sattva* is our means of knowledge. *Rajas* doesn't know anything, because it is too busy keeping the world moving. In case you didn't notice, things are never the same from one millisecond to the next. And *tamas* is a black hole with reference to knowledge; it absorbs light and obscures things. So the business of knowledge is left to *sattva*. Knowledge appears in *sattva* as thoughts. Animals don't have civilizations, because they don't think. Yes, knowledge is built into them by *Isvara* in the form of the macrocosmic *sattva*, but they are not aware of it as such. It seems like they are using it, but it is actually using them. They are just intelligently designed programs. But when it comes to human beings, whatever glory we deserve is due to our ability to think, for which we can thank *sattva*. Of course you can successfully argue that if we couldn't consciously think, we would be spared at least one perennial and nasty human institution: war.

Most of our thoughts have to do with *samsaric* preoccupations, manipulating life to get what we want and avoid what we don't, but it need not be this way. We can gain knowledge for its own sake or for the sake of our highest value: freedom from dependence on objects. In the case of enlightenment, knowledge is the only way because we are already free. And since self-knowledge is so subtle and counter-intuitive, we need a preponderance of *sattva* or we won't succeed.

Consequently, if you will recall, we defined the Yoga of the Three Gunas as adjusting the relative proportions of *sattva* with reference to *rajas* and *tamas* so that *sattva* dominates the subtle body, making the job of inquiry easy, assuming a strong commitment to self-knowledge.

7. Dispassion, Discrimination, Humor

Sattva is the mother of dispassion and discrimination. Desire and fear disturb the mind and distort perception of reality, but *sattva* is a steady, bright reflection of awareness that sees things as they are. Seeing the upside and the downside is dispassion, and dispassion makes discrimination effective. Awareness of life's ironic contradictions is responsible for humor, one of *sattva's* signature qualities.

8. SECURITY

Rajas creates tunnel vision, and *tamas* blurs reality, obscuring the big picture. *Sattva* provides panoramic awareness and the ability to reason effectively. When you understand what is happening, worry is not necessary, because you can confidently respond.

9. EPIPHANIES

Insight, intuition, inspiration and epiphanies are due to *sattva,* which confers an ability to see things clearly and to look deeply into things. It is responsible for alertness and intellectual brilliance. Consequently it makes discrimination, dispassion and sustained commitment, three cornerstones of inquiry, possible.

Sattva is responsible for varieties of spiritual experiences because it reveals the Self. Experience of the Self reflected in the subtle body is indirect knowledge, but is valuable nonetheless if it is properly contextualized by scripture.

10. CONSERVATION

Sattva endows the mind with discrimination. Consequently a *sattvic* mind understands the value of values. Therefore it inclines the mind to maintain values appropriate to self-inquiry and eschew those that aren't. *Rajasic* and *tamasic* values require no maintenance, because they motivate the doer unconsciously. A *jiva* motivated by bad values who makes a connection between its suffering and its values does so only when *rajas* and/or *tamas* are momentarily dominated by *sattva.*

11. COMPLETION

Rajas produces a life full of unfinished projects and missed or botched opportunities. When a powerful desire interrupts the mind in the middle of an activity, *rajas* tends to initiate a new project without finishing the project at hand. A *sattvic* mind, however, is peaceful and unconstrained by time, so it is capable of completing a project or resolving an issue before it moves on to the next. Therefore it is reliable and persevering. *Rajasic* people tend to be unreliable owing to the scattered, time-sensitive quality of their minds. They are often unable to keep appointments and to keep projects on schedule.

12. CREATIVITY, INVENTIVENESS

Creativity is basically allowing *Isvara* to provide ideas that the *jiva* is not capable of thinking when its mind is dull or disturbed. When *sattva* predominates, the *jiva* becomes creative and inventive.

13. CONFIDENCE

Firm knowledge is only possible when the mind is predominately *sattvic*. When you are certain about what you know and don't know, you are completely confident. Individuals with predominant *sattva* are cheerful and fearless.

14. MORALITY ~ THE VALUE OF VALUES

The moral dimension of reality is called *dharma*. Inability to appreciate the value of *dharma* is one of the great failings of modern spirituality. Somehow in that world of misfits and rebels, the dos and don'ts, shoulds and shouldn'ts are too closely associated with moralistic parents or simple-minded religions to be taken seriously, so the baby went out with the bathwater. Spiritual or worldly, ignore the moral dimension of reality at your peril.

It's true that original pure consciousness is free of good and evil, but it is the only and ultimate moral value because, as mentioned above, it is always good. It is "that knowing which nothing else need be known, loving which nothing else need be loved." It is the basis of *samanya dharma*, the universal moral values reflected in the *sattva*.

Dharma is based on *sattva*, non-dual knowledge, but *dharma* is as *dharma* does. When I was young, the society had more than a passing interest in manners. Most of the major papers employed nationally famous manner mavens who discussed the finer points. Sadly, manners have gone by the wayside. Manners convert *rajas* and *tamas* to *sattva*, which acts as a buffer between you and raw emotion. If someone is aggressive toward you, and you respond in kind, the likelihood of a successful outcome is close to nil. If you respond to someone from a *tamasic* state of mind, the likelihood of a successful outcome is very low. If you are polite and self-effacing, it will invoke *sattva*, an accommodating energy that increases the likelihood of favorable results.

Please refer to Chapter VIII for a discussion of the following *sattvic* values: resolution of inner conflict, self-confidence, steadiness, non-violence, fearlessness, honesty, non-stealing, cleanliness, purity, order, simplicity, accommodation, commodiousness, charity, gratitude, anger resolution, renunciation, austerity, restraint, self-control, satisfaction, service to the teacher, compassion, chastity, humility, modesty, forbearance, straightforwardness, truthfulness, absence of ownership, love of solitude, completion, appreciation of time, dispassion toward sense and emotions, and unswerving devotion to God.

The Downside of *Sattva*

Rajas and *tamas* obstruct bliss, which is the nature of the eternal, ever-present, ever-experienced Self. On the other hand, *sattva* doesn't obstruct it, but allows it to be experienced. We can't call *sattva, rajas* and *tamas* thoughts exactly, although thoughts are *sattvic, rajasic* or *tamasic*; they are states of mind which last much longer than thoughts. Occasional *rajasic* thoughts may zip through a *sattvic* mind, but unless the volume is substantial, they won't speed up the mind and convert the *sattva* into *rajas*. A *tamasic* thought, in keeping with its nature, may leisurely creep into a predominately *sattvic* mind, but can be easily recognized and ignored in favor of the creative peacefulness of *sattva*. Because the *gunas* are states of mind, they don't last. They continually morph into one another. When the volume of zippy *rajasic* thoughts or lazy *tamasic* thoughts increases to a certain point, they overpower the *sattva,* and the mind becomes predominately *rajasic* or *tamasic*. A *sattvic* thought may appear momentarily in a *rajasic* or *tamasic* mind, but it will quickly be overwhelmed by the thoughts created by the dominant *guna*.

As noted earlier, the idea that enlightenment – freedom from the mind – is experiential is based on a failure to discriminate *sattva* from original pure consciousness.

It's an honest mistake because pure *sattva* perfectly reflects the bliss of existence/awareness. So people who experience it mistake it for the Self and try to maintain the experience, which is impossible. This lack of discrimination accounts for the plethora of aging, jaded cynics hanging around on the periphery of the spiritual world, whose minds were *sattvic* when they were younger but who weren't qualified for Vedanta and gravitated to energy-transmitting *gurus* who had no teaching apart from their own experience of the *sattva*. Because of this they were unable to properly contextualize their spiritual experiences and develop *sattvic* lifestyles, in which case their inspirational epiphanies may have led to self-inquiry. But without proper understanding they became *tamasic,* and discrimination did not develop, thus preventing them from appreciating non-duality. They are nice enough, but live in the glory days of past epiphanies, worshiping dead experiences and false *gurus*.

When *rajas* is dominant, the intellect becomes a doer, but when *sattva* is present, the intellect becomes a knower, and the idea "I know" is superimposed on the Self. Knowing is quite wonderful, but no matter what you know, you know very well that you are not omniscient, so there is always a sense of limitation with knowledge. In fact the more you know the more you become aware of what you don't know. Such is the nature of the duality. So when *sattva* is predominant, you know that you are happy. But the implied meaning is "I will soon be unhappy" because as soon as you feel happy you want it to last. An enlightened person, knowing what it means to be the Self, may say, "I am happiness itself," but never, "I am happy." Whereas happiness is the Self, the Self is not happy. It is self-aware, effortlessly self-experiencing bliss, which is not transactional and is not a state of mind.

ENLIGHTENMENT SICKNESS

Sattva has no downside in itself. It is just pure reflected awareness. Humans rightly prize knowledge, virtue, beauty, freedom, love and happiness. When the mind is *sattvic* we experience one or all of these qualities in ourselves, and the tendency to identify with them is overwhelming because they bring security, pleasure, fame, respect, power and wealth. However, claiming ownership of the *sattvic* qualities when in fact they belong to *Isvara* can stall your spiritual growth for lifetimes.

If you think you are very wonderful because you are enlightened, know that while you were reveling in the wonder of a *sattvic* experience, real or imagined, *tamoguna* snuck into your mind and deluded you. Once you start creating *karma* under the aegis of the "I am enlightened" idea, your growth stops because humility, a *sattvic* quality, disappears when the idea "I am finished" appears. To you the thought "I am finished" means that you have achieved the ultimate state, but it actually means that you have become a frozen, enlightened automaton, devoid of creativity and spontaneity, and probably infected with any number of ugly conceits, especially arrogance. No matter how much adulation you are able to attract from the world, your *rajasic/tamasic* mind continues to generate negative *karma* until one fine day *Isvara* pulls the plug and only you are fooled anymore. You are never finished, because you never began.

Rajas ~ **Pure Duality**

Most of the qualities of *rajas* have been explained above in various contexts, so this section adds a few points that were not properly unfolded before. It also provides a comprehensive list of keywords and phrases that will help you cement the knowledge in your understanding.

CHARISMA

One meaning of the word *rajas* is "to shine." People in whom *rajas* predominates tend to be attractive people. The projecting power of *rajas* combined with the reflective power of *sattva* creates an aura of energy and power, charisma, which can be a great blessing insofar as your desires will be satisfied if people are attracted to you. But it may very well become a curse because getting what you want may not always be what you need. There are two ways to suffer: getting what you want and not getting what you want.

The glow of romantic love is *rajas* and *sattva* creating attractiveness. But as you age you tend to become less attractive as *tamasic* habits deposit layers of dust on the mind, dimming the glow.

SELF-CONFIDENCE

Because success in any field requires consistent, intense application of energy, *rajas* can also create a legitimate sense of self-esteem, particularly if it is guided by *sattvic* ideas. However, if it is supported by *tamas,* failure is likely because *tamas* deludes the intellect and ruins discrimination.

EXCITEMENT

When you are *tamasic* you are completely unimaginative, bored, boring and perhaps depressed. But eventually *rajas* injects some dynamism into your tired mind. When its spiky energy wakes you up and you emerge from your dark hole into the light of day, a cup of espresso in hand, everything feels fresh, new and exciting!

Responding quickly to every rapidly evolving situation is challenging and maybe even a little scary considering where you came from, but it feels good, like a roller-coaster ride. You feed on the energy of other *rajasic* types, basically every other overstimulated human, and you're off and running. "More! Better! Different!" is your holy *mantra*. Your speech is infected with hyperbole. Everything is "Incredible! Fantastic!! Terrific!!! AMAZING!!!!" So you overdo doing and you want the excitement to last forever.

But your whole experience is false. Nothing is amazing, and you are not amazing at all. You are the same needy, uninteresting person you always were; you are just caught up in the emotion of *rajas,* which only feels good because *tamas* feels so depressing.

Unbeknownst to you, *tamoguna* is gradually taking over your subconscious because the unforgiving stream of activities is wearing out your primary and secondary instruments. They can only go so far so fast without generating a serious *tamasic* funk. Thank God: if the *rajas* kept up, you would die.

Rajas is the *guna* of desire and passion. Passion is intense and sustained involvement with long-term objectives, unlike desire, which is intense and momentary fascination with immediate goals. Properly balanced with *tamas* and inspired by *sattva*, passion accomplishes great things, worldly and spiritual. If your life is little more than a web of stultifying thoughts, emotions and habits, the only way out is to develop enough *rajas* to destroy the lethargy. Tempered with the *sattvic* qualities of discrimination and dispassion, burning desire for liberation is an essential prerequisite for success on the path of inquiry, which is, sad to say, fraught with many obstacles.

Many become wildly excited when they discover Vedanta because it explains reality clearly and reveals a reasonable way out of *samsara*. However, when the excitement starts to wear off, you may wonder what's next. "I know the world isn't real and that I am the Self, so what do I do now?" If you find yourself bothered by this thought, you did not take time to appreciate the value of Vedanta beyond removing your ignorance. If you understand the actual implication of complete, fully actualized self-knowledge, the excitement will slowly be converted into a lifelong passion, one that will enrich you beyond measure.

When you get too excited by something, including Vedanta, it is easy to lose the plot, which often takes the form of a heartfelt desire to teach others. If you were awakened to this great knowledge at the hand of a traditional Indian *guru* with knowledge of the scriptures in Sanskrit, you may think that to be an effective teacher you need to know the scriptures in the original, which is not true, although it can't hurt. Sanskrit is an incredible language, unique in the world of languages, so it is easy to transfer your excitement to Sanskrit. To teach Vedanta properly, you need to understand the science, not the language.

The science is knowledge, and knowledge can be expressed in any language. You certainly can study Vedanta, but Vedanta is not meant to be studied unless you understand that you are the subject. Because you are looking ahead to the day when you will become a great teacher and enlighten the world like your *guru*, you learn the basics and you convince yourself you are the Self and are free, when in fact the ego has co-opted the knowledge. You don't realize that "I am the Self" is the fifth stage of enlightenment and that there are two more to go: negating the doer and moving beyond *sattva*. You are sure you have negated the doer, but you haven't, because the knowledge and the excitement belongs to the doer. Sometimes it takes five or ten years to realize your mistake.

Rajas Is Required to Gain Experience and Knowledge

We have focused so much on the downside of *rajas* that you may get the idea that it is the enemy. Like *sattva* and *tamas*, it is just a value-neutral energy on the macrocosmic level. But when the *jiva* appears in all its ignorant, dualistic glory with an acute sense of incompleteness, *rajas* may very well become a problem. At the same time, it is one of life's valuable building blocks, essential for transforming matter into inanimate and animate forms. Yes, I need *sattva* for knowledge and satisfaction, but I need *rajas* to work out my *karma*. I need to pursue objects, material and spiritual. This pursuit is only painful if the *jiva* lacks discrimination and uses its energy to serve exclusively material ends.

Rajas Creates Time and Duality

Whereas *sattva* generates a feeling of timeless peace because it reflects the timeless peace of existence, *rajas* creates time in the form of desire and fear. Our likes and dislikes create an artificial sense of separation from the world that manifests as a feeling of "time." When you look into the idea of time rationally, you see that it doesn't exist objectively except as a concept to make life in the transactional reality more efficient. The transactional reality is the objective world, which operates in accordance with strict laws that can be expressed in terms of time. Although the *jiva's* body exists in the objective dimension and is subject to its laws, its mind is affected by desire and fear, which create a subjective sense of time. When its desires are being met, time flies; when they are not, time hangs heavy on its hands.

For example, you do not like shopping but you have to shop. It's your day off and you are happily excited about meeting your friends at the beach. You stop at a busy supermarket on the way for a few beachy things: suntan lotion, a hat, beer and deli sandwiches. There is a fat lady with a big shopping cart standing in the middle of the aisle talking with a clerk. It is difficult to pass. It angers you that she is so inconsiderate and that you have to ask her to move aside. You see yourself as a considerate person and like yourself for it. You think she should know better and show some courtesy. You get to the bread aisle, but the hot dog buns have been moved. It is a big store and you can't see a clerk. The prices are high, so you expect the store to have clerks available to serve you.

You remember that the fat lady was talking to a clerk, so you retrace your steps, but the fat lady is gone and the clerk is nowhere to be seen. Your anger increases. After roaming many aisles, you finally find the buns next to the hot dogs. But your preferred organic brand is out of stock. You are mindful of your health, so you have to examine the other brands to see if they are chemical-free, sugar-free, etc. It takes time.

More frustration. It seems like your shopping is taking forever, even though you have only been in the store five minutes. After more self-imposed indignities, when you finally get to the checkout there is a long line. The checker's shift just ended, so the line stops moving. It seems you have been in the store for an eternity.

Owing to *rajas*, the ego feels a need to plan. Plans are fantasies because what is to come has already been decreed by *Isvara*, the causal body. The Creation is a huge machine, and *Isvara* can't afford to wait till the last minute to make up Its mind as to which of many quadrillions of results should manifest in a given situation, so right at the beginning it thought the whole thing out, cranked up its almighty will, banged the whole production into existence and sat back to watch the play.

Transcendental boredom hangs heavy on *Isvara's* hands, and it needs entertainment. Even though *jiva* is a mini *Isvara* clone, it isn't omniscient, so unlike *Isvara* it doesn't know what will happen. It knows something will happen and it has its desires, so it fantasizes.

For instance, you are an entertainer and you are planning an event. Many people will be there. It is your chance to shine, so you start dreaming of all the possible ways you would like to experience the event. The very fact that you are invested in your plans means that you are setting yourself up for failure because things never go as planned.

Or things may generally proceed as you imagine, but *rajas* makes you so sensitive and vain that even one small glitch can ruin the whole thing for you. Your costume may malfunction and the audience may be treated to a bird's-eye view of your private parts. The embarrassment, the shame! But the audience greatly appreciates it because your song and dance is a little lifeless owing to the fact that you unwisely stayed up partying till four in the morning the night before. Motivated by your desire for appreciation and recognition, you had imagined enthusiastic, adoring applause, but they were applauding for the wrong reason – you made a fool of yourself.

Well, you didn't really; *Isvara* set it up that way for its entertainment. *Isvara* also has to take care of the results of the audience's need to be entertained. They spent fifty bucks, hauled their sorry asses to the venue and they need to get their money's worth. They would have been satisfied if your performance had been up to par, but it wasn't. *Isvara* didn't want to disappoint them – the needs of the total come first! – so it factored in the malfunction just for laughs.

In fact somebody was filming with their smartphone and posted it on the internet where it went viral. You wanted fame alright, but not this kind of fame. Henceforth, people smiled when you walked into a room, but they weren't smiling for the right reason. Poor ego. When you plan without the knowledge that *Isvara* is the giver of the results, you are setting yourself up for disappointment, which you may sort of know, so you try to envision all the contingencies, which invariably leads to more desiring, planning and doing. You never reach the end of wanting things to turn out as you imagine they should.

Before we take up the next topic and spare you further enlightenment on the topic of *rajas*, here is a more or less complete, some might say depressing, list of *rajasic* qualities, although it is probably better to think of it as a helpful warning. Since *rajas*, coupled with its *tamasic* twin, is the curse of the modern era and seemingly no one is immune, it might be helpful to chant it religiously in this manner: "*Om*. Salutations to *rajas*! *Rajas* causes *tamas*. *Rajas* creates doership. *Rajas* distorts perception. *Rajas* skews assimilation. *Rajas* causes attachment. It makes me needy and dependent. It makes me greedy. *Rajas* makes me stubborn. *Rajas* projects. Projection prevents success. *Rajas* causes confusion. It makes me feel big sometimes and small at others. *Rajas* causes anxiety. It causes anger and rage. It makes me impulsive and undiscriminating. It tempts me to cut corners. It makes me manipulative. It makes me lie. *Rajas* causes stress. It makes me feel overwhelmed. *Rajas* causes boredom. It makes me seek variety and novelty. *Rajas* makes me waste energy doing just to do. My leg shakes and I fidget. *Rajas* makes me argue and quarrel. It makes me miserly and covetous. *Rajas* makes me jealous. It makes me envious and competitive. It causes hatred. O *Rajas*, my master, which of your deadly sins have I forgotten? *Om shanti*."

Tamas ~ The Dark Energy

Rajas is anxiety, and anxiety is painful. If you don't have enough willpower and knowledge to transform *rajas* into *sattva*, you will default to some form of *tamasic* activity to manage *rajas*.

The obesity epidemic sweeping the developed world today is *tamoguna* in action, for which you can thank your parents. When your *rajasic* wailing drove them crazy, they did not give you a hot cup of coffee or fit you up with a vegan burrito liberally slathered with habanero hot sauce; they shoved something fat or sweet into your mouth to shut you up. The rest is history.

NORMAL ANXIETY IS NOT NORMAL

Tamas makes your mind dull, and a dull mind doesn't feel anxiety. The absence of anxiety therefore feels like a positive *sattvic* state, but it isn't. The *rajasic* anxiety is still there, hiding under a cloud of sloth. As you keep suppressing your emotions in this gross physical way, it builds up and breaks out in some form of painful *karma*, like diabetes or cancer. Unless something fortuitous happened to make you reasonably self-aware between your childhood and now, there is a straight line between your present view of emotional management and the views of your loving but unevolved parents. So if you manage your *rajas* with *tamas* in this manner, don't count on a happy life. In fact if *tamas* is your predominant energy, your life is basically wasted. So even though you do feel momentarily good when you eat sweets and fats, inquiry reveals the sad fact that this upside of *tamas* is in fact a downside, to wit: worry about your health and obsession with your body image, not to mention increased food cravings.

RIGIDITY, INFLEXIBLITY, CONTRACTION

Dullness is one characteristic of *tamoguna*, rigidity is another. *Tamas* is fear in action. If you automatically look for what can go wrong in every situation instead of what can go right, know that your mind is predominately *tamasic*. If you are the proud possessor of every conceivable type of insurance, know that you score zero on the non-duality index, because ours is a benign universe, set in motion by a compassionate God. We can easily make the case that the insurance companies are the most non-dual institutions in the world because they are betting that good trumps evil overall, which it does. If there were any real contest, we would all be packing weapons and looking over our shoulders every minute, life would grind to a standstill and we would find ourselves living in nightmarish, dystopian societies.

Yes, there are places like South Sudan and the Congo where fear is the predominant energy, but they are exceptions, not the rule. There are always exceptions because anything is possible in *Maya*. When you bet on non-duality, you win. You needn't grow up in a poverty-stricken, high-crime area in an inner city to enjoy the curse of *tamas*. Good, middle-class people – and even rich people, God forbid! – suffer from the fear syndrome, their behavior ossified into contracted, stultifying patterns that prevent them from taking advantage of the opportunities inherent in every situation. Fear may be smart in a given situation, but it is not smart in every situation, because the macrocosmic *gunas* are always in motion. A *sattvic* situation generally demands a creative, open-ended response, not a *rajasic* reaction or *tamasic* avoidance. So if *tamoguna* compels you to invariably react negatively or if you are too rigid to think on your feet and supply the energy the situation demands, you will respond inappropriately and miss an opportunity to grow.

If you are a *samsari* and want to keep your *tamasic* friends, don't ask them to do anything more strenuous than fiddling the controller on their Xbox or hoist a cold brew toward their lips. A *tamasic* situation demands a *rajasic* or *sattvic* response if you are an inquirer. For instance, you spent a lot of money on a nice house "as an investment" and you became attached to it. However, after a few years, the economy turned down and the bottom dropped out of the market.

You saw the writing on the wall, but *tamas* made you sentimentally attached, and by the time you were ready to let go of the attachment, your house was worth far less than what you paid for it. Oddly, nobody wanted to buy it at your price, even though *rajas* projected the idea, which you swallowed hook, line and sinker, that it was "worth" every penny you are asking.

Tamas is appropriate between the hours of 10:00 pm and 6:00 am, and occasionally throughout the day, but it is inappropriate when the daylight hours require *rajas* and *sattva* so you can think on your feet and respond effectively.

Habits are not bad. Life is nothing but habits. But habits are not good in themselves; they are a means to an end. So when your mind is racing so fast that you don't realize you are doing two things at once, you are in the danger zone. At one point during my misspent youth I realized that cigarettes were smoking me and alcohol was drinking me. On the conscious level, my mind was so wrapped up in some project that I was unaware that I had smoked forty cigarettes during the day. The pain of the addiction was much greater than the pleasure of smoking, so I set to work on those *vasanas*. It took two years of hard work and knowledge from an extraordinary experience to purify these habits.

FEAR OF LOSS

A *vasana* is a simple tendency or impulse to pursue or avoid something. A *samskara* is a group of similar *vasanas* that over time becomes virtually indelible and generates a predictable pattern of behavior which defines a *jiva's* basic response in every situation. Duality means that there are two basic ways to look at a given situation. You can, for instance, see the outcome of actions as a gain or as a loss. If *sattva* is your dominant *guna*, you will have a sunny personality and tend to take a dispassionate stance when something happens because you will see the upside and the downside. Black swans are white swans for you. Any way it works out is interesting.

If *rajoguna* is dominant, every situation is an opportunity ripe for exploitation. *Rajasic* types accomplish a lot because they aggressively engage life, but they also suffer much because their greed compromises their discrimination; it makes the intellect hurriedly and uncontrollably hop from one thought to the next rather than judiciously drill deep into every idea looking for the upside and the downside. They can't wait to spring into action, so they skimp on research and get to work immediately. They skim and skip over the details because the imagined result is so tantalizing they can almost taste it, even though it may not manifest for years, unlike *tamasic* types who know well that the devil is in the details and dither away endless opportunities contemplating the downside of every thought to insure against mistakes.

Rajasic types often believe they are "lucky" and tend to be endowed with a false sense of self-confidence, particularly if they have experienced a modicum of success. Black swans are non-existent for them. They will consistently underestimate the time required to get a given result, because they never took the time to think things through. They will exaggerate the benefits and minimize the losses inherent in any plan because deep down what they really want is to be busy.

If you are proud of your ability to multitask, know that you are caught firmly in the jaws of the *rajasic* crocodile. *Rajas* makes sitting alone in a quiet room a torturous exercise; without distractions the torrential cascade of thoughts drives the mind crazy. When a desire comes up, you act it out immediately to remove the pain. But you don't know that desire is painful, owing to the fact that society touts it as a great virtue.

Rajas will cause you to dump your life savings into a project calculated to make you rich in no time, it will roll up your sleeves for you, make you hit the deck running – how exciting! – and cast your endeavors in dramatic, heroic terms. "I'm doing it for my family! I'm saving the world!" More than one-third of all business start-ups fail, but you do not see yourself in that cohort – until you are.

THE LORD GIVETH AND THE LORD TAKETH AWAY

Whereas *rajas* makes the mind think in terms of gains, *tamas* inclines it to think in terms of losses. The mind under the spell of *tamas* is all black swans. If you lost a loved one when you were young and your subtle body was predominantly *sattvic*, you will suffer, but your sunny disposition will re-emerge after a while. However, if your subtle body was *tamasic*, the sense of loss will likely become a *samskara* and color your basic response to the world for a very long time, often until the day you die. There will be an expectation of pain and loss in every situation. You may be quick to laugh at others, but you will never laugh at yourself. Life is serious! Both little and big things will be cause for concern, and you will rarely relax.

You may have subordinate *sattva* and enjoy yourself when you are cloistered away in the relative security of your own home surrounded by loved ones, but your extremely sensitive mind will worry about your reputation, your appearance, your money, your family, your health, global warming – what have you. There is always a sense of incipient dread; things might go "wrong." And they do, not because they necessarily do, but because that is how you see things. Right and wrong, likes and dislikes are projections.

NORMALIZING THE ABNORMAL

A deep, negative, fear-based *samskara* is virtually impossible to recognize because it invariably hides behind a mask of normality. Every extremely trivial and seemingly necessary action seems completely reasonable, but it isn't. The *samskara* is like a monstrous parasite hidden in your bowels, living off your energy. You probably think that your sense of powerlessness is a psychic remnant, the consequence of an ancient event that will eventually end one day or that is amenable to some special therapy, but you don't realize that you are unsuspectingly feeding the monster every time you refuse to question and neutralize the small daily fears that feed it.

They seem to be generated by your current situation, but they aren't. Parasites are very clever, humble, patient and secure. They have no need for recognition and allow you just enough life to give you hope. They survive on your belief that the fear is real and rue the day you discover that it isn't. Just as they patiently suck the life out of you, you need to patiently suck the life out of them, but you can't, because you think they are real. Every time the fear rears its reasonable head you need to dismiss it. And when the fear arises that renouncing fear is unreasonable, you need to cling to the knowledge of who you really are and dismiss the fears as they arise. Day in and day out, thought by thought, you must starve the *samskara*. It is the only way, but the goal more than justifies the effort.

Four years ago I had quintuple bypass surgery, and the doctors put me on statins meant to prevent a heart attack, which seemed to be a reasonable idea. Yes, I got a new lease on life, but I soon discovered that living on statins is akin to driving your car with the emergency brake on. Whereas previously actions just happened without effort, now I had to consciously exert my will to accomplish things.

During my inquiry into this situation I realized that every pill I took to prolong my life was actually making my life miserable because every pill was just a tiny, friendly dose of fear. Fear contracts you. It puts the brakes on your energy. If someone had told me that I was living in fear, I would have dismissed their statement out of hand. I am completely fearless. But I had unwittingly picked up the world's fear of death because it masqueraded as a reasonable, life-enhancing therapy. As soon as I saw it, I threw away my statins, acting became effortless and my life returned to wonderfully normal.

FEAR IS NOT SMART

The only way to know if a particular something is capable of extending your life would be to know when you were "supposed to" die before you tried it and to remain conscious when you actually died so you could see how much "time" you saved or lost.

You may resort to statistics to justify your fears, but statistics never identify the likelihood that an individual will experience a particular event, only what the cohort will tend to experience and, needless to say, nobody is a cohort. In every case study there are many individuals that enjoy all the risk factors but never suffer the event. How do you know that you are not one of those, in which case you could profitably chuck your life-extending technique in the trash? It is equally likely that even if you take your statins religiously you may very well die of a heart attack "before your time" because many members of a particular cohort experience the unwanted event even though they exhibit none of the risk factors.

Sattvic fear, precaution, for instance, is smart, but fear is not smart, because reality is basically benign and you can maximize your chances for a long, happy and fearless life with *karma yoga* by eliminating fear, and *guna* management, which eliminates most risk factors.

Because there is no way to know what will happen, quality of life is essential. So the question should be, do I want my primary instrument continually disturbed by fear and desire or do I want a calm, peaceful mind?

Tamas has an emotional upside because duality pervades all three *gunas*. The first is sleep, a very positive state. In fact the feeling associated with the state of pure *tamas*, when the subtle body is merged in the causal body, is bliss! Bliss is the sustained, reflected experience of the Self, unbroken by discrete experiences, i.e. thoughts and feelings and the presence of individuality. It is the grandaddy of all positive emotions.

The popularity of the no-thought theory of enlightenment is an attempt to mimic the sleep state in the waking state based on the fact that pure *tamas* is bliss. Here is the seemingly logical reasoning, keeping in mind that bliss is the desired result of every action: if there are no thoughts and bliss in deep sleep, the absence of thoughts is bliss. Therefore I should get rid of my thoughts in the waking state and enjoy bliss. It's a nice, tidy little argument, but it doesn't take reality into account. If *Isvara* intended for individuals to not think in the waking state, It would not have created ignorance, *jivas,* free will and the law of *karma* in the first place, because you need thoughts to create and destroy *karma*.

Thinking is a very valuable tool if it is backed by knowledge of reality. Otherwise, it is a problem. But getting rid of the mind isn't the solution. The mistake is in assuming that correlation is causation. The absence of thoughts does not cause bliss, even though bliss is more likely to be experienced when thoughts are absent. That said, bliss is present even when the mind is thinking.

In any case, you can argue that the feeling of security belongs to *sattva* because *sattva* is knowledge, and the feeling of security is based on the knowledge that everything is always fine, appearances to the contrary notwithstanding, but *tamas* plays a role too because *tamas* inclines the mind to secure things. It makes the mind practical. You work hard so you can pay for your insurance. *Rajas,* on the other hand, is too busy acquiring stuff to invest the time required to keep it. I know a man who was making obscene amounts of money but was too excited by the money-chase to take care of the small stuff himself or to hire *tamasic* people who enjoy dealing with life's humdrum details like taxes, customer complaints, etc. One fine day the government came calling and, well, the outcome was not fun.

If you don't take time every day to pay quality attention to your spouse because you are turning the wheels of commerce and industry, you will come home one fine day to find a note on the door informing you that your spousal duties have been unilaterally terminated and a letter in the mailbox from an attorney.

PERSEVERANCE, DETERMINATION

It's hard to say whether perseverance and determination are *tamasic* or *sattvic* qualities, but both are extremely useful because there are many setbacks as you work on your *gunas*. Bad habits, the effects of the *rajas/tamas* complex, are only defeated with a persistent determination to apply the teachings in every situation. Instead of resisting change, a dedicated inquirer should steadily welcome it.

SMART FEAR

Smart fear is an oxymoron if ever there was one. However, insofar as fear keeps your nose to the grindstone and you ground your ideas in reality, practicality may be considered one of the upsides of *tamas*. Nonetheless, since intelligence is one of *sattva's* most salient characteristics, it might profitably be classified as a *sattvic* use of fear.

TAMAS CAUSES ATTACHMENT

The degree of attachment to objects is directly proportional to the degree of insecurity caused by ignorance of one's wholeness. Because of attachment, a *tamasic* mind is miserly. Hoarding is a fine example of a mind deeply shrouded in *tamas*.

TAMAS PRODUCES DELUSION

False values are born of delusion, which in turn is caused by *tamas*, ignorance.

TAMAS GIVES RISE TO FANTASIES

Tamas makes the *jiva* too lazy and incompetent to achieve real-life results, so it resorts to fantasies.

TAMAS CAUSES CONFUSION

If you can't determine the nature of a situation because your mind is dull, you are unable to respond appropriately.

TAMAS CAUSES DISTRUST

Tamas conceals the true nature of things. You can't trust what you can't see.

TAMAS CAUSES GULLIBILITY

A *tamasic* mind is easily exploited because it lacks the curiosity needed to investigate things. It is anti-intellectual.

TAMAS CAUSES CONFORMITY

An undiscriminating mind incapable of thinking for itself is subject to group pressure. If you can't think properly, you blindly follow rules and formulas, even when unnecessary. Predominately *tamasic* people are like sleepwalking automatons.

TAMAS CAUSES RIGIDITY

Tamas is responsible for an individual's failure to adjust to changing circumstances. Predominately *tamasic* people are forever disappointed owing to missed opportunities. Rigidity is the enemy of innovation and timely responsiveness.

TAMAS CAUSES RESISTANCE

Predominantly *tamasic* individuals are stubborn to a fault. They are like pit bull terriers. If they get a grip on something, they won't let go. They will fight to the death.

CONSERVATISM

Conserving what is good is conservatism. This value may be profitably listed under the topic of *sattva*, insofar as knowledge of what is good and true implies an understanding of the value of goodness, which is only possible if *sattva* is predominant. It can also be seen as a *tamasic* value because *tamas* inclines the individual to value things simply because they have stood the test of time. Time is not a good criterion for determining value, because bad values are also eternal. This value inclines an individual to nostalgia and sentimentality, two characteristics of *tamas*.

ABSOLUTISM

A *tamasic* mind lacks subtlety. It sees life in black and white. It is too insecure to be wrong, so it is always "right." It does not appreciate diversity, so it tends to find a single cause for every problem: the government, the economy, sugar, religion, immigration, conspiracy, minorities, what have you. It needs a villain. There is one answer for everything: Jesus, veganism, lower taxes, free healthcare, a wall on the border, etc.

LITERALISM

Tamasic people live in a subjective, one-dimensional universe. They cannot appreciate irony, symbolism and implied meanings. They take everything literally.

TAMAS CAUSES LOW SELF-ESTEEM

Tamas is a heavy, dark energy that vibrates with negativity. It is gullible and readily accepts the voices of diminishment society plants in the mind. It makes you weak and saps your resolve. Signature thoughts: "I'm not good enough – I can't – I'm a victim – see my scars."

TAMAS CAUSES NEGLECT

A *tamasic* mind doesn't do what should be done when it should be done. It dithers and procrastinates. It causes parents to withhold love from their children, a primary cause of low self-esteem. Neglect is an unconscious form of cruelty.

TAMAS CAUSES SELFISHNESS

It is myopic, only concerned with itself. Consequently it is incapable of giving and receiving love. It's the source of miserliness.

TAMAS PRODUCES LUST

Tamas is responsible for addictions and compulsions. Because it drains your energy and makes you weak, you cannot stand up to your fears and desires, and easily become addicted to pleasure.

AVOIDANCE, DENIAL, PROCRASTINATION

Because *tamasic* minds are so dull, the inherent lethargy of their words and actions are unknown by them, so they are in a more or less constant state of denial and downshifting, which causes those under the influence to shirk responsibility and avoid necessary confrontations.

PERVERSION, SCHADENFREUDE

Masochism. When the mind is extremely *tamasic* it may become perverse and take pleasure in pain. Or it may take pleasure in the misfortune of others. Or it is contrary for the sake of contrariness: "You say yes, I say no. You say goodbye, I say hello."

CRUELTY

Cruelty is a characteristic that might as well belong to *rajas* insofar as it is projected pain, but insofar as *rajas* and *tamas* are basically inseparable, it can also be classified as *tamasic* because you have to be extremely insensitive to inflict pain on any living being.

MELANCHOLY

Persistent fantasizing causes persistent disappointment, which leads to the formation of a *samskara* that colors the *jiva* with melancholy.

Chapter X
How *to* Cultivate *the* Gunas

AT THIS POINT the nature of the *gunas* has been unfolded. But the best part has been left to this chapter. Changing the *guna* composition of your mind on a daily level is where the proverbial rubber meets the road. You already realize this if your life is centered around your practice because *karma yoga* and self-inquiry gradually produce predominant *sattva*. But what if you have yet to move your practice from the periphery to the center of your life? If so, this simple chapter will set you on your way to a more *sattvic* and peaceful daily existence.

1. Really Accept the Zero-Sum Nature of Reality

It's easy to pay lip service to the zero-sum nature of reality, but truly assimilating its meaning sets you on the royal road to freedom and non-dual love.

There's a good reason the apparent reality is called "the rat race." Western society's version of the rule governing the race is pretty clear. We can probably agree that it goes something like this: pay to play to win for you and yours. No matter that "coming out ahead" means there are more losers than winners, but since nobody likes losing, its better to play to win. You score points by acquiring value in the form of results and objects that the media praises: prestigious college degrees, important jobs, smart, sexy spouses, big houses and scads of gratuitous perks and luxuries. Sad to say, however, when the winners take stock they realize that they paid dearly to get what they thought they wanted. There are no free lunches here.

Have you ever wondered why – oddly – winners tend to be no happier over all than losers? We know this, yet we keep on playing. Even the unhappy big winners didn't become disillusioned because they were unskillful or unlucky but because they were playing the wrong game in the first place. They were trying to find value in a world that is value-neutral. All value is projected value, and once one's projections are no longer sustainable in light of the facts, we become unhappy.

An inquirer is uninterested in the world's stuff. He or she understands that winning lies in the way you play the game. The rules of life, *dharmas,* are built into the fabric of life by an intelligent ordainer and they benefit those who follow them. If you read the "Care and Handling" tag on your subtle body, it says "indulge *adharmic* living at your own peril." Why? If you are chasing the world's shiny baubles, you are playing against yourself!

Knowledge of this fact makes you a player in the real game of life. And the winners from self-inquiry gain an unlimited, imperishable reward. If you follow *dharma* and manage your *gunas* for predominant *sattva*, your life will become the perfect vehicle for self-realization and you will get to share your bounty – limitless bliss – with others. Game over.

2. Connect Actions and Their Results

What we can't see is always impacting our lives. For instance, the relationship between action and its results is rarely straightforward. Wouldn't it be nice if we got the result we wanted immediately when we performed an action? If *karma* was that straightforward, it would be easy to determine which actions to avoid and which actions to do. If every time I said a bad word I found ten dollars, my speech would be nothing but expletives. What if every time I shot the basketball it went through the hoop? If there was no uncertainty, I might as well be an insect.

Karma is seriously nuanced and paradoxical, sad to say. What you see is not what you get. Well, it is but it isn't. Every action produces short-term seen results and long-term unseen results. The short-term results I know, the long-term results I don't know until the chickens come home to roost. Most of us agree that good deeds should go unpunished. But because of the law of unintended consequences, sometimes I get pain for doing the right thing. For instance, it's not right to injure my body, so I stop smoking and my self-esteem comes roaring back. But immediately I become irritable as my smoking *vasana* starts a war with my resolve, a war that can last months or years. Yes, in the long run it's a good thing to do, but in the short run it is fraught with pain.

I'm having a very angry fight over alimony with my cheapskate husband, who is hiding the loot, and I scream, "I'll kill you, you son of a bitch!!!" This thought is probably a valuable escape valve for me, but if I keep thinking it, I may find myself sitting in a jail cell for twenty years because the hitman botched the murder and I got caught. Coffee is great short-term to get rid of morning *tamas,* but once the addiction sets in, the mind becomes a disturbed, *rajasic* mess. Bad habits are the ego's bread and butter. Take one away and you are asking for trouble.

At the same time, if you don't get rid of them, you keep suffering. In case it escaped you, the point is: doing an expedient, feel-good action is not always the way to go. The solution? Carefully think through every action intended to relieve boredom or stress. If common sense or scripture says that an action or thought that you favor does not conform to *dharma*, do inquiry until you see the logic. And don't put on your lawyer's hat and try to find the loophole.

For instance, scripture recommends celibacy for inquirers. Why? Because sex creates a binding *vasana* overnight. If your subtle body is predominately *tamasic-rajasic* with a little *sattva*, and you are inclined to fundamentalist religion, you will probably take the advice literally. So you repress your sexual needs until your mind becomes hopelessly distorted. But if you are *tamasic-rajasic* with virtually no *sattva* and no spiritual inclinations, you will let the sex *vasana* do the thinking, reject the idea outright and end up lustfully wallowing in the narcotic realm of the senses until you contact an incurable disease.

Or if you are *rajasic-tamasic* with little *sattva* and spiritual inclinations, you will decide that you need to get married because sex is sanctioned for married couples. So you get married and end up copulating like a rabbit. Seven kids later you may rue the day you didn't have enough *sattva* to think of marrying for love.

If *sattva* is playing handmaiden to *rajas*, and you have enough *sattva* to reason, you will not take the prohibition literally. You will grab your lawyer hat and start arguing. Does that really mean no sex? Maybe, but maybe not. Hijacked by desire, your *sattva* might reason like this: "Sex is a God-given state of mind. I don't think, 'I'll be sexy,' and then the feeling comes. The feeling comes automatically in certain circumstances, so *Isvara* is telling me to have sex. Since I'm a good devotee I will do what *Isvara* wants and worship *Isvara* with *tantra yoga*. It's the fast track to non-dual devotion."

If you are predominately *sattvic*, you will not be quite so interested in satisfying your desires. You will be, obviously, but you won't immediately fall afoul of *tamasic* or *rajasic* reasoning. You will try to figure out the intent behind the rule, consider your circumstances and come up with a workable solution.

When asked about the sex issue or any other apparent sin, my *guru*, who was a celibate holy man, used to say "sin intelligently," meaning be mindful of the upside and the downside. Sex per se is not a self-insulting action, although it may become one. Don't repress, don't indulge. Maintain your dignity and occasionally throw the dog a bone. Or you might redefine chastity as a respectful attitude toward the opposite sex, which removes the problem altogether.

Life is a set-up. There are no free lunches. You cannot beat it, meaning there is no solution here. You may think you are very lucky and that you deserve all the good fortune coming your way, but you can be sure that one day the downside will kick in and take the smile off your face. At the same time, you have no choice but to work out your desires on your way to freedom, so you need to be brutally honest and carefully determine if the long-term result moves you closer to your goal.

If it will, you need to be willing to suffer in the short-term for long-term benefits. If the long-term result of an action is *sattvic*, it is *dharmic* for you. If it is *rajasic*, determine if it is practical, and if it is, do it. *Rajasic* actions do not necessarily produce good or bad *karma*, but they can be a great waste of energy. If it's *tamasic*, forget it unless you have insomnia.

3. Apply the Opposite Thought

Although we touched on this idea above, we will develop it further in this chapter. In Chapter VIII we discussed the characteristics of the three primary energies, concluding with a daunting list of negative *tamasic* qualities.

It is obvious to anyone with a modicum of discrimination that any or all of these qualities are not going to transform themselves into positive qualities overnight, although they can be purified. It is also true that the number-one reason people find themselves involved in spirituality is directly related to positive and negative states of mind imposed by *guna*-driven values. It is equally true that human beings are like animals: they don't like to waste energy, and so they look for the most expedient solution. It turns out that while the expedient solution is, well, expedient, it is not always the best. Fantasy comes into play here because it is easier to imagine that willpower alone or some fancy spiritual technique can produce transcendence and render the *gunas* impotent rather than to opt for the realistic approach, which is to invoke *Isvara*, roll up your sleeves and get to work transforming negative qualities into positive qualities until you have a sparkling, *sattvic* personality.

As you can see, there is a certain creativity and leeway allowed in this type of spiritual play. So if you suffer:

+**Attachment:** Attach yourself to the teachings. Don't let go of the truth.
+**Distrust:** Distrust your thoughts and feelings until they have been subjected to rigorous inquiry.
+**Conformity:** See that all your thoughts conform to scripture.
+**Rigidity:** See that all your actions rigidly conform to *dharma*.
+**Inflexibility:** Inflexibly practice devotion.
+**Resistance:** Stubbornly resist the siren song of your worldly desires.
+**Conservatism:** Don't piss away energy in sense pursuits. Save good habits.
+**Absolutism:** Absolutely assert your true identity when fears and desires disturb you.

◆**Literalism:** Take the prohibitions and injunctions in the scripture literally.

◆**Neglect:** Neglect gratuitous desires.

◆**Selfishness:** Selfishly cling to the self.

◆**Miserliness:** Hoard solitude.

◆**Addiction:** Become a Vedanta junkie.

◆**Compulsions:** Feel compelled to inquire and pray daily.

◆**Avoidance:** Avoid gratuitous desires, bad company and *tamasic* food.

◆**Denial:** Deny limiting thoughts, such as "I am small and inadequate."

◆**Blame:** Blame *Isvara* for factors beyond your control.

◆**Perversion:** Take pleasure in learning from egoic suffering.

◆**Greed:** Greedily save time and invest it in self-inquiry.

◆**Hatred:** Hate selfishness, sloth, ignorance and deceit.

◆**Guilt:** Feel guilty for not doing your best spiritually.

◆**Jealousy:** Jealousy guard your purity.

◆**Envy:** Envy the wisdom and purity of great souls.

◆**Boredom:** Become bored with your ego's relentless fears and desires.

◆**Covetousness:** Covet solitude.

◆**Anger:** Be angry every time you forget who you are.

◆**Waste:** Don't waste time in frivolous pursuits.

◆**Lust:** Lust after the truth.

◆**Infidelity:** Cheat on your worldly self.

◆**Despair:** Despair when your mind is not thinking of *Isvara*.

◆**Grief:** Grieve when your love is not flowing to the Self.

4. Develop a Simple, Devotional Lifestyle

What you have and what you don't have may serve as the basis of success in a materialist society, but for those of us who love freedom, our possessions and social roles do not make us who we are. Scripture says that a non-conforming lifestyle prevents liberation. A non-conforming lifestyle is suitable for the pursuit of *samsaric* ends: security, pleasure, power, fame, worldly knowledge, etc. but these lifestyles don't work for contemplatives, simply because they keep the mind extroverted.

A conforming lifestyle is a simple lifestyle that enhances contemplation. The spirit of renunciation is the backbone of simplicity. If your temperament is *rajasic* and you want *moksa*, you will have to cultivate this spirit because it is not native to *rajoguna*, much less *tamas*. *Rajas* is desire born of a perceived lack of wholeness. So people afflicted by *rajas* lead busy, cluttered lives. If the doing-thought is central to your identity, fine, but don't expect self-inquiry to work unless your predominant doing is self-inquiry. Difficult as it may be to contemplate, something has to give if you want to grow. It helps if you are utterly fed up with the unyieldingly disappointing hand dealt by *samsara*.

The degree of difficulty in letting go is directly proportional to your attachment to *samsaric* pursuits. If you're in a loveless, boring relationship out of habit and fear of loneliness, the relationship has to go, one way or the other. Relationships are attractive because they purport to solve a problem or problems. You left your spouse without getting to the root of the conflict and a new somebody came along that promised to remove loneliness but actually buried the hurt behind an initially exciting relationship.

Or your marriage, which was quite sexy and interesting at first, eventually fell into the doldrums. One day an abandoned dog wandered onto your property, which awakened tender, loving feelings, but you bonded with the dog, not with yourself or each other. Problem solved, but not really, because the original issue is still there. So when your second husband or wife leaves you or your dog dies, getting a third wife or a new pet is not the way to go. *Isvara* has just provided you with an opportunity to cultivate the spirit of renunciation. That empty space that is initially flooded with grief is the perfect environment for self-inquiry.

Self-inquiry builds self-esteem like nothing else because you are doing the right thing for your Self. Loveless relationships are a symptom of low self-esteem. You need self-confidence to manage your *gunas,* and you can salvage it from the wreck of a *tamasic* mind by cultivating the spirit of renunciation.

Certain minimal relationships, possessions and activities are necessary to sustain life, but a significant fraction of them are completely useless as far as contemplation is concerned. So inquiry is looking into and dismissing the excuses we make to avoid simplifying our lives. If you find yourself using the word "need" in place of the word "want," your spirit of renunciation needs a bit of work. If you define luxuries as necessities, your spirit of renunciation needs a bit of work. Actually, you need to contemplate this *koan*: less is more. If you can crack the code, you're well on the way to a simple, devotional life.

It is not within the scope of this book to discuss the details of a *guna*-managed lifestyle, only to unfold the knowledge of the *gunas* and give you a feel for how they work psychologically.

5. Monitor Your Diet

It may be news to you, but food-knowledge is an essential part of a *guna*-managed lifestyle. Most of us do not realize that we do not choose our food; our food chooses us. If you think about it, your parents conditioned you before you had any say in the matter. And your parents got their knowledge from their parents, who got it from theirs, etc., etc. Not to put too fine a point on it, their idea of food had little or nothing to do with nutrition. It was based on the power of food to manage emotions. They wanted their darling little bundle of joy to be happy so it would love them.

Once you were off breast milk, which was good if your mother was healthy, they observed that a sweet or a fatty food shut you up momentarily when you were emotional. The issue here is taste, not that sweets and fats are necessarily nutritionally detrimental. You learned that if a food tastes good, you feel good. This of course is obvious and not the kiss of death, but it does not mean that using food to manage your emotions is wise.

Taste Is Out

Taste is not a good criterion for food selection, because it is completely conditioned by factors out of your control. From Mom and Pop you learned that taste is everything because pleasing tastes made you feel good, but one thing your parents didn't know or didn't choose to know: you will eat whatever is in front of you if you are hungry. Dogs in America turn their noses up at rice and vegetables, but dogs in India wolf them down. When you are a baby, you don't know what food is supposed to taste like. If you're fed grasshoppers you will develop an attachment to them because nutritious foods satisfy you. Birds, the most *rajasic* and healthy critters on earth, eat them for breakfast, lunch and dinner. I have traveled to many countries and I am always impressed by the joy that people get from eating absolutely disgusting things.

You also probably don't know that a food that doesn't taste particularly sexy at first can easily become an attachment if it provides you with excellent nutrition – because the body knows what is good for it. If you listen solely to your emotions, you put your health at risk. Big Food knows about the taste thing. As soon as you can trundle off on your own with lunch money in your pocket and enter the sacred portals of knowledge, you pass a shiny mechanical mom who will happily dispense the *tamasic* food of your dreams: a Snickers bar, a Baby Ruth or a Coke.

Poverty Consciousness (*Tamas*)

And, unless you came from a rich family with an understanding of nutritional science, the cost of food was an important budgetary consideration, so your parents shopped for price. The cheapest foods, thanks to factory farming – carbohydrates like wheat, soy and corn – are not necessarily unhealthy, but if your diet is based on them, you can cheerfully look forward to what in the nutritional world are referred to as one or more of the many diseases of civilization.

Before we wind up the lifestyle idea, here is an extremely short and incomplete introduction to the food *gunas*: surprise, surprise, a *tamasic* diet creates sleepy, dull thoughts and depressing feelings. A fried steak is *tamasic*, although it may not be unhealthy, because it has many essential nutrients. Bitter, hot and astringent foods are *rajasic*. They activate the *pranas* and the mind – think coffee – and cause *rajas*. They are not inherently bad. Sugar is *sattvic* because it produces bliss immediately, a *rajasic* burst of energy in the short run and *tamas* post-digestively. Too much sugar – think alcohol – causes depression. Most fruits and vegetables are *sattvic*. Flesh foods like fish and chicken are relatively *sattvic*, although meat is *tamasic* overall. Fresh foods are *sattvic*.

Methods of cooking are *rajasic*, *tamasic* and *sattvic*. Storing and refrigerating foods reduces *sattva* and *rajas*. Suggestion: monitor the post-digestive effect of foods and evolve a diet that maintains consistent *sattva*.

6. The Media

Lifestyle is a lot more than food, although a glance at the bodies of many Americans makes you wonder. It is relationships, food, money, recreation, sex, work and sleep. Extreme wealth and power allows individuals in so-called advanced societies freedom from certain basic insecurities, like food, clothing, shelter and war, and produces discretionary income that should be used wisely, not frittered away on inadvisable pursuits. It also seems to produce a surfeit of boredom and a mind-numbing lack of imagination.

If materialist people had rich inner lives, the gargantuan media machine would shrink to the size of a pea. One might persuasively argue that the media is one of the most – perhaps the most – pervasive and powerful institutions in society.

Media is a society looking at itself and talking about itself. Therefore, since materialist societies are almost exclusively *rajasic* and *tamasic*, our minds are gorging on *rajasic* and *tamasic* fare every waking hour. And the implication? If you want to *sattva*-size your mind, go on a media fast. Well, take it easy; to date no modern human has ever managed to go cold turkey. Gradually wean yourself off this intellectual junk food.

7. Stop Talking About Yourself

Modern non-dualism, which burst on the spiritual scene about twenty years ago and which is known as Advaita or Neo-Advaita, has a few things right:

(1) you are not your body, (2) you are limitless consciousness and (3) you are not your story. It seems obvious when you think about it, but it's not how most of us live our lives. For starters, most of us believe that we are people. But what exactly is a "person," a term as nebulous as the word "America." It is an identity, a collection of thoughts cobbled together on the basis of various experiences, real and imagined, positive and negative, that happened to the body and mind stretching back to birth. But no matter how interesting it is, it never describes you or equals you. What happened to your body and mind prior to now has nothing really to do with you. The longer you pretend that it does, the longer you remain in ignorance.

Conclusion: stop talking about your not-self. That person is not you. A person is consciousness enveloped in a material sheath. Thinking that a conceptual person is real is a mistake, and talking about it as if it were real only serves to compound the mistake. If you need an identity, you can confidently claim to be limitless, ever-free, ever-experienced, ever-present consciousness, assuming you know what that means in terms of the body and world you indifferently witness.

Here's why you are not real: the you that you think you are is a new you after every experience. Nobody, including you, knows what it actually is, because it is impermanent. You meet a high school chum at your thirtieth class reunion, but you can't even recognize the body, much less the person inside. You have nothing in common anymore, because he's not the same person. Yes, everyone needs an identity, but your identity should be based on something real, not on a bunch of thoughts.

When you see the word "I" appear in your mind, you should examine it carefully to see what it refers to before you open your mouth. If it's the "not-you," you can profitably delete it and all the words that modify it, unless you know that it is not real, as it will only serve to reinforce the belief that you are small and inadequate.

8. Analyze Your Speech

Analyze subconscious thought patterns that reveal duality. From the outside, everyone is enlightened until they start speaking. As soon as they complete a few sentences, the ignorance starts to appear in the form of the implied meanings of words. The statement "you look good today" implies that you did not look good yesterday, otherwise the speaker would have unambiguously said "you look good." From it I can infer that the person who said it has conflicting feelings about me, since he or she has identified my "I" with my appearance, of which it is free.

Similarly, the causal body, the source of self-ignorance, expresses self-ignorance every waking hour. For instance, if you say, "I think the president is a fool," which may or may not be true, depending on your definition of foolishness, you are actually saying that the Self thinks. It doesn't. It is actionless awareness, and has no mind or senses. The statement "I'm enlightened" is a classic example of self-ignorance because the Self, the "I," was never unenlightened. It always effortlessly knows itself.

If you are blessed with strong desire to know who you are, a simple lifestyle, a *sattvic* mind and have completed the listening phase, there is perhaps no more effective tool than speech analysis.

Chapter XI
Beyond *the* Gunas

....

*"When the subject sees no doer other than the gunas and knows
itself to be other than them, it is free."*
~ Bhagavad Gita

....

Conversion of the *Sattvic* Personality

IF REALITY IS only non-dual, there is no world, and if there is no world, there are no people, and if there are no people, then there are no free people. Reality is non-dual, but non-duality is peculiar in that it has two orders, *satya* and *mithya*. When self-knowledge dawns, the apparently real dimension, where people exist, does not dematerialize never to be seen again. If it did, there would be no enlightened people, because there would be no dimension for them to inhabit. So the person and its body doesn't experience any change when you know who you are, a fact that does not attract many to Vedanta, because most people join the spiritual crowd because they want to be different people.

If you want to be a different person, manage your *gunas*. You can be just about anything you want in the *mithya* dimension if you understand the *gunas* and how they work, and if you do actions appropriate to your goal. If you want to be a real demon and get on the FBI's Most Wanted list, cultivate as much *rajas* and *tamas* as is humanly possible, and your chances of success are high. If you want to be an intelligent, kind, giving person, cultivate *sattva*, and it will make you saintly. Most good people would settle for sainthood because they more or less like themselves and are more or less liked by everybody.

Saints are highly evolved, but they are not totally pure *jivas*. A *jiva*, an individual, is always a mixture of positive and negative characteristics because *jivas* exist in duality. So saints have problems. The Self is totally pure, but it is not a *jiva*. You only gain purity by understanding that you are the Self. A free person is problem-free. So if you evolve a predominately *sattvic* personality, there is one more step: liberation.

Yes, freedom is the nature of the Self too, and if there is only the Self, then everyone is free and there is nothing for anyone to do as far as freedom is concerned, but this chapter is about a free *jiva*, one that was previously bound. In

143

a way, it's better to be an animal because there is no freedom problem for animals, who take reality as it is. They don't suffer, because they don't think about what's happening. They don't feel bound. Bondage and freedom are *mithya* issues alone.

For freedom you need to evolve *sattva* because it focuses the mind on the bliss aspect, which makes the *jiva* happy. When it is happy for no reason apart from its enjoyment of reflected bliss, it doesn't need to do things to become happy, so it doesn't initiate projects with happiness in mind. At the same time, *sattva* makes the mind very intelligent and subtle, so it easily understands the difference between what is real and what isn't. If you understand that objects are only apparently real, you will not pursue them, and your binding *vasanas* will begin to relinquish their hold on you.

Conversion of binding *vasanas* into preferences is liberation, transcendence of the *gunas*. All situations are acceptable. Life situations are neither good nor bad; they just are. And because the Self is bliss, life with all its joys and sorrows is a constantly entertaining "so what?"

The body, mind and intellect never become ever-free consciousness. They are always inert. Only the relative proportions of the *gunas* can be changed. So the only way to change things lies in a radical change in your understanding of matter. Once you understand the nature of matter, you accept it because there is no way to change it. Your "equipment," as Chinmaya Swami called it, is an ever-changing, decaying instrument, so you learn to detach and dis-identify with it. You can't do this until you understand the teachings on *Isvara*, because they make it crystal-clear that *Isvara* is causing action. The *guna* teaching is the teaching on *Isvara/Maya* because *Isvara* is the three *gunas*. The three *gunas* are not teachings on consciousness, the subject. They are teachings on *prakriti*, matter.

Knowledge shifts your identity to consciousness, where it belongs, and the teaching on *Isvara* makes it simple for you to turn over ownership and controllership to *Isvara*, where it belongs. In case you have a doubt, the last statement in clear, simple English means you don't own anything, you don't control anything and you don't love anything but the Self. Yet no one is excluded from your love, because everyone is you.

A free person accepts the law of *karma* completely. He knows that what happens is completely up to the factors in the *dharma* field and the momentum of his past actions, and does not want anything to be other than what it is.

The following is a list in no particular order of the qualities of a free person in terms of action, knowledge and love. If you can tick all the boxes, you are free, although the presence of one benefit implies the presence of the others. It is not intended for the evaluation of others, only for self-knowledge; nobody knows what another person knows, thank God.

1. COMPLETE SELF-SATISFACTION

A self-actualized person enjoys an awareness that includes the perception of body, mind, senses and surroundings, but remains unidentified with them. The knowledge "I am limitless existence/consciousness" has been fully assimilated because there is no sense of separation, and a palpable sense of satisfaction that expresses as love for everyone and everything, including the flawed ego. The non-dual devotee is free of object-love (and equally free to love objects) because non-dual unconditional love is its own fruit. This devotee is even greater than a noble person who knows intellectually that he is the Self. The fully self-actualized person is completely satisfied with himself, his ego, his equipment and his situation in life because he is the ever-full, overflowing Self.

2. FEARLESSNESS, IMMORTALITY, SECURITY

Fear comes when you are alone and you believe there is a second entity. Fear doesn't arise when you are everything. Fear also comes because life is uncertain, does not always give us what we want and takes away what we value, particularly our lives, our most valuable possession. A free person is free of fear because he experiences no difference from the immortal Self. He or she is totally secure.

3. CONSTANTLY EXPERIENCES NON-DUAL LOVE

If reality is non-dual and love exists, which it does, then the Self is non-dual love. A person who is established in self-knowledge is unconditionally loving.

4. ALL STATES OF MIND ARE THE SAME

Free people are not averse to any state of mind, nor do they long for any state of mind, because they know the *gunas* control every state of mind.

5. MIND ABIDES IN THE SELF

The mind, your primary instrument, has no nature of its own. It becomes whatever it pays attention to. If it is paying attention to an emotion, for instance, it becomes emotional and moves here and there. If knowledge locks it on the Self, it experiences constant bliss. It remains effortlessly focused on the Self because the Self is immortal love, and it knows *mithya* love is a pale reflection of the real thing.

6. Unconditional Peace

The mind, the primary instrument, is the container of thoughts. It is non-separate from the Self. So it is not disturbed when thoughts enter and leave. The *Bhagavad Gita* (2.70) says: "All experiences enter the mind of a wise person through the senses, but they create no agitation, because a self-actualized person is full in himself, just as rivers pouring into the ocean do not disturb it. Because he is full, he is not a seeker of experience." All thoughts that spring up from the causal body have been rendered non-binding by self-knowledge, so they don't disturb the mind.

7. Every Experience Is a Pleasure

When you ask for something, you may not get it, but when you discover the fullness that is your nature, even though you don't want or need anything, every experience is a pleasure. If the non-dual devotee desires at all, the desires are born of fullness; they are not tainted by self-interest and they only bless the world. Although they have nothing left to accomplish for themselves, non-dual devotees tirelessly act for the well-being of the world.

Comparing non-dual devotees with *samsaris* with reference to pleasure, Swami Paramarthananda says: "Their attitude is one of controlled enjoyment. It is like the difference between rash driving and fast driving. Fast drivers control speed. If a child were to run across the road, this driver would be able to brake in time. Rash drivers are accident-prone because the excitement of speed controls them. The wise person's enjoyment of sense pleasures is like fast driving, whereas the ignorant person's enjoyment of pleasure involves risk."

8. No Sense of Ownership

Enlightened people understand that their bodies, minds and relationships belong to the world. All wives and husbands, mother and fathers, children and relatives are theirs.

9. No Sense of Doership

Isvara, the *gunas*, are doing everything. Free people do not feel that they are doing anything; they impartially observe things happening. The *Bhagavad Gita* says: "The one who sees actionlessness in action and action in actionlessness is wise and has done everything that is to be done."

A self-actualized person knows that when something is happening in the apparent reality, nothing is happening to the Self. A person sitting in a stationary train that has been traveling in one direction feels as if he is moving when a train on an adjacent track moves in the opposite direction. Self-actualization is total identification with the unchanging, non-experiencing witness, not with the thoughts coming and going. From the station's point of view, nothing is happening. The feeling "I am doing" is caused by superimposition of action on the actionless Self. The "I" is always free of action.

"Actionlessness in action": a boat on the horizon rapidly moving out to sea seems to be unmoving to a person standing on the dock from which it departed. Although nothing is apparently happening, something is happening. Freedom from action is not attained by doing nothing, because the equipment is constantly active. A self-actualized person is engaged in the world like everyone else. "I am not the doer" means "I am limitless, non-dual, actionless awareness." It is not a statement about the body, mind and intellect. A liberated person is free of the need to act while acting. The apparent person is actually the Self and lives differently in the body from the rest of us. There is no feeling of gender. He or she is happy with what comes by chance and doesn't want to be like anyone else.

10. SEES NO DIFFERENCES

"A free person sees no difference between a lump of gold and the excreta of a crow." He or she sees the essence of everything because desirable and undesirable things are non-separate from the essence of everything.

11. COMPASSION

A free person sees beyond people's delusions and knows everyone is the Self, no matter what they believe, and experiences an active empathy with everyone.

12. CONTROL OF THE SENSES

Speaking of free people, the *Bhagavad Gita* says: "If a person is able to withdraw the sense organs from the sense objects like a turtle withdraws its limbs, his or her knowledge is steady." Because we live in the world, our senses are always active. But because sense contact with objects produces pleasure, and pleasure creates *vasanas* for more pleasure, *jivas* can easily become prisoners of their senses. A self-actualized person is not averse to pleasure. The verse implies that the sense organs of the liberated are connected to objects. But self-knowledge saves the day because a self-actualized person knows that the pleasure that comes from objects is actually a faint, reflected, transient blip of the eternal bliss of himself. Experiencing one's Self as the source of that bliss neutralizes the bliss *vasanas*, but not the bliss. Therefore a self-actualized person enjoys any experience and can step back from any experience.

An enlightened person knows that as he experiences objects – life is just a constant experience of objects – he is experiencing the existence, the consciousness, the happiness and the love of himself alone. He says, "When anyone experiences love, it is me experiencing love." As it says in the *Bhagavad Gita* (6.29): "He sees all beings in the Self and the Self in all beings."

13. Free of Longing

Because a free person always feels complete, desires for particular circumstances – pleasure, for instance – dries up. When desires are absent, anger is also absent because anger is just obstructed desire. There is no escape from pleasant and unpleasant circumstances, because the enlightened person lives in the *dharma* field. But circumstances have no effect, because they belong to the field, not to the Self. If a soldier realizes who he is in a war zone, his life is still dangerous, only his relationship to the danger changes.

Withdrawal from pain does not involve willpower for either the enlightened or unenlightened alike, but withdrawal from pleasure is difficult for *samsaris*, because they feel incomplete. Free people do not celebrate pleasure, although they experience their fair share because they are not attached to it.

14. Total Dispassion

If you are full, you are the meaning of your life. If you are the meaning, what use is there for objects? They don't validate you; you validate them. Objects for the non-dual devotee are purely utilitarian; they cannot add to the fullness he experiences. This non-dual devotee is like Teflon: nothing sticks to him or her. This is not to say that free devotees do not have desires, only that acting on them is completely optional. In addition to the power to act and to know, the power of desire is a sacred and glorious gift from God only bestowed on human beings. If you interview a dog about its plans, it may bark a couple of times and then run off to sniff the behind of another dog. But human beings can pursue extraordinary, world-enhancing objectives.

15. Well Looked After

A non-dual devotee cannot improve himself. He is someone who knows that he is everything and everything is him, so there is no self-loathing or room for injurious thoughts and actions. All his relationships are love relationships. If I am love and everyone is me, what's not to love? These devotees enjoy wonderful lives because everything required to survive in the transactional reality comes from apparent others. If others are loved, they cannot help but love back – *Isvara's* law of *karma* – so the world takes excellent care of such devotees.

16. Alone, but Never Lonely

The desire for love in this world is born of duality, but there is no duality for a free person. He or she is the ever-alone Self, but aloneness is not loneliness. It is "all-oneness." It is unconditional, effortless self-love that does not come and go.

17. Follows Dharma

Scripture encourages self-actualized people to follow *dharma*, which implies that they are free to violate it. Despite the fact that a self-actualized person is unaffected if he violates rules, he should dot his "i"s and cross his "t"s. Enlightened people can be compared to children. If a child violates the rules, the child is not arrested. Similarly, when a dog walks against the traffic signal, the police don't write a ticket. Rules are relevant only where ego is involved. A non-dual devotee has transcended the doer-enjoyer entity – he is the Self after all, so even if he violates the rules, he will not accrue good or bad *karma*. As it says in *Tattva Bodha* (38.1): "Knowledge destroys future *karma*, and the self-actualized person is not affected by it, just as a lotus leaf is not affected by drops of water sitting on it."

Three Reasons They Follow Dharma

A. Even though a non-dual devotee is not afraid of bad *karma*, he or she nonetheless follows the rules, not out of a desire for good *karma* or fear of punishment, but out of compassion for the worldly order.

B. Until you know who you are and your knowledge is firm, scripture is your protection. But once you know, the roles are reversed and you need to protect scripture.

C. If we don't regularly polish our brass and silver valuables, they become tarnished. Similarly, a non-dual devotee is advised to remain conversant with the scripture for the protection of his or her own self-knowledge.

18. Not Required to Follow Dharma

A self-actualized person is not, however, required to follow *dharma*. To restrict him in this way would limit his freedom because he is the Self, and the Self is beyond *dharma* and *adharma*. Sometimes the interests of *dharma* are sustained by *adharmic* acts, so you may observe a self-actualized person occasionally breaking the rules. The question concerning action, which takes place in the *dharmic* order, is always about knowledge. What does a person know when he is acting?

A self-realized person knows that *Isvara* is the doer but may have *vasanas* left over from his stay in ignorance. He will not develop new *vasanas*, because the ignorance is gone, but he still has to experience the effects of ignorance as the momentum from his past actions, although he is not identified with what happens. So discrimination is necessary for the self-realized until the effects of ignorance are reduced to ashes in the fire of self-knowledge. The self-actualized person knows that *Isvara* is the doer, but does not need to discriminate, because his actions are automatically aligned with *Isvara's* desires and because the effects of ignorance have been burned by self-knowledge.

So selfish desire and action are no longer an issue. However, since both *dharma* and *adharma* are *Isvara,* and his equipment belongs to *Isvara,* he may occasionally act *adharmically* in service of *Isvara.* His *adharma,* however, will be minimal because his mind is predominately *sattvic,* and *sattva* inclines the mind to *dharma.*

19. LIFELONG GRATITUDE

The wise non-dual devotee's gratitude to *Isvara* is undiminished through his life, even though his debt has been canceled by self-knowledge. Without *Isvara,* the teacher and the teaching, he would have been unable to experience the constant blissful freedom of non-duality.

In the *Taittiriya Upanishad* (part 3, *Bhriguvalli,* verse 10), the non-dual devotee's song is recorded: "Bliss! Bliss! Bliss! I am food and I am the eater of food. I am the one that brings the food and the eater together. I am the first-born of the true, the eternal and immortal. I am the immortal center, prior to the gods. Whoever hands down this knowledge preserves it. I am luminous like the sun. He who knows this attains the aforementioned results."

20. PURIFY HOLY PLACES AND JUSTIFY THE SCRIPTURES

Dualistic devotees leave their sins in the holy places, but non-dual devotees purify holy places because they are non-different from God. Whatever they do blesses the world. Their dwellings become pilgrim centers. Their lives lend credence to the scriptures.